By God's Intelligent Design: The Individual's Workbook

APOSTOLIC
driving vision

PROPHETIC
elevating truth

TEACHING
adding perspective

EVANGELISTIC
inspiring action

PASTORAL
nurturing care

Adam L. Janowski

A 7-Week Study of Spiritual Giftsets and Fivefold Purpose

Published by ABContrast Press
Horseheads, NY
(ABContrast.com)

First Edition: October 2025

ISBN **979-8-9930516-2-8** (paperback)

Library of Congress Control Number: **2025922019**

Table of Contents

Part 1:

Successfully Studying By God's Intelligent Design

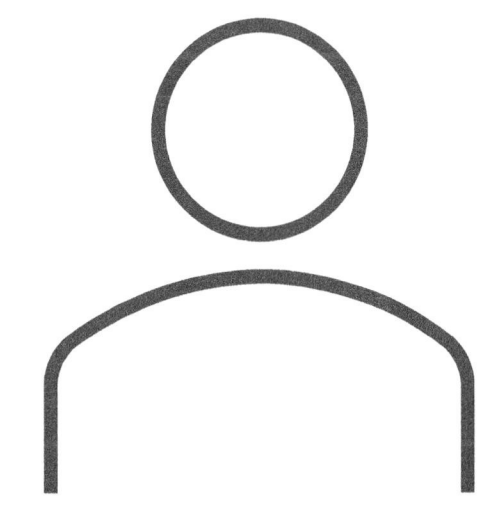

Your Adventure Continues

Studying Your God-Given Design

Welcome to the builder's adventure. This workbook is your companion guide for the journey to answer one of life's most profound questions: "*What is my purpose?*" Think of these pages as the blueprint for an adventurous construction project – building a design portfolio of *you*. **You are the explorer discovering the divine plans, and also the builder tasked with bringing them to life.** Together, we will journey through the unique "rooms" of your design's intent.

Its purpose is to propel you beyond simply knowing about spiritual gifts and into **discerning**, **developing**, and **deploying** them. The principles you will learn shape your service in ministry, form your home-life interactions, guide the exchanges within your closest relationships, and define your influence in professional or organizational settings. **The Intelligent Designer Placed Divine Purpose Within You!**

Soon, you'll be able to confidently inspire others by recognizing and affirming the spiritual appointments you see in them. **This becomes an effective way to build up fellow Christians and a natural bridge for engaging everyone else.** Understanding this design is your key to unlocking a more fruitful and fulfilling experience in every aspect of your life.

Prepare Your Heart for Conversation

While a shared study has its own rewards, the solo path offers a unique space for unfiltered introspection, allowing you to wrestle with these concepts in a deeply personal conversation between you and God. We'll be right here with you in spirit.

As you read, continually ask God to reveal how He has uniquely equipped you. Embrace this powerful opportunity for deep reflection, prayer, and honest self-assessment as you engage with the material. Be open to new revelations in His timing, while seeking healthy interactive exchanges with the world around you.

The Seed and the Soil

Just as a wise builder first prepares the ground before laying a foundation, we must cultivate the *good soil* of our hearts. Jesus' Parable of the Sower is a guide to this essential site preparation. **Your spiritual gifts are seeds from heaven, each containing the divine potential for a fruitful, life-giving harvest.** God's intent is that every seed should flourish, yet as the parable warns, many never reach their full potential. <u>*Why?*</u> All too often, this is because the soil conditions of our hearts and lives are unprepared. (Matthew 13:1-23; Mark 4:1-20; Luke 8:4-15)

◇ **The Hardened Path:** Some gifts fall on ground that has been compacted and hardened by constant traffic. The seed cannot penetrate this surface; it simply lies exposed. This is the heart that hears the call but does not understand or receive it. Because the talent finds no place to take root, the enemy (like the birds in the parable) comes to snatch away what was sown.

◇ **The Rocky, Shallow Soil:** Other gifts fall on a thin layer of dirt that covers a bedrock of stone. These talents may sprout quickly, received with immediate joy, and a new ministry or talent springs up with promise. However, there is no depth for roots to grow to support lasting development. When the sun beats down, the initial excitement withers instead of enduring hardships.

◇ **The Thorny Overgrowth:** Other gifts are sown among thorns. Here, the seed takes root and the plant begins to grow, but it is not alone. Jesus identifies the thorns as earthly concerns: the deceitfulness of riches, and the desire for other things of this world. The given ability is slowly choked out, its vitality drained by worry, ambition, and distraction until it becomes unfruitful.

◇ **The Good Soil:** Finally, some gifts fall on good soil. This is the heart that has been tilled and prepared. It is a heart that hears, understands, and accepts the endowment, holding it fast with patience and perseverance. Here, the seed is **not** stolen, scorched, or suffocated. It is cultivated, allowing it to take deep root and produce a magnificent harvest for the Sower's Kingdom – **thirty, sixty, or even a hundred times what was sown.**

Embracing this seven-week study is evidence of your desire to cultivate good soil. It is a practical guide to breaking up the hardened ground of indifference, digging out the rocks of shallow commitment, and pulling the weeds of distraction – so that what God has planted in you can flourish beyond measure.

Stewarding What We've Been Given

This exploration begins by shifting our focus from what we lack to the incredible potential God has already placed within us. **Too often, we fall into one of two traps:** we either worry about the abilities we don't have, or we become envious of the gifts we see in others and their ministries.

Jesus directly addresses these tensions in His parables.

He told of a landowner who paid all his vineyard workers the same wage, regardless of their start time. When some cried foul, the landowner replied, *"Is it not lawful for me to do what I wish with what is my own?"* (Matthew 20:15; also see vv.1-16). Likewise, in the parable of the talents (Matthew 25:14-30), the master intentionally varied what was entrusted to each of them, **concerned only that they were faithful with the portion they were assigned.**

Like those wages and talents, God distributes His gifts as He sees fit. **Our purpose is not to compare our portion with our neighbor's, but to faithfully steward what heavenly wisdom has given each of us.** This is about discovering the potential God has planted within you and learning how to faithfully serve your Kingdom purpose.

How to Prepare for the Journey Ahead

This path is a powerful opportunity for deep self-reflection, prayer, and honest assessment as you engage with the material. To get the most out of this experience, it's important to prepare not just your materials, but your heart and your study environment.

Adopt the Right Approach

◇ **Allow Yourself Some Grace:** As you uncover your strengths, you will also be invited to look at your *Shadow Side* potential. **It's essential to approach this basic part of humanity without judgment.** Seeing your struggles clearly is not a reason for shame; it is the first step toward freedom and wholeness in Christ. **Remember, God's grace is always bigger than our** *shadows.*

◇ **Embrace the Role of the Builder-Explorer:** Your goal over the next seven weeks is discovery, not just diagnosis. Pay attention to the concepts that energize you and the ones that challenge you, as the **hints about your design are often found in your natural reactions to the reading.** This framework is not a box to confine you, but a blueprint and a map to guide your builder's adventure. Be equal parts curious and honest with yourself.

◇ **Maintain a Prayerful Posture:** This journey is, above all, a spiritual one. Before each reflection time, begin with a simple prayer. **Ask God to** *"quiet your heart, give you an honest view of yourself, and reveal the beautiful and complex way He has intelligently designed you for a unique purpose."* Allow the Holy Spirit to whisper new truths and open your eyes to the fullness of the King's domain!

Create Your Space of Intentionality

Don't let this important work get lost in the hustle of daily life. Designate a specific time and place for your weekly studies – perhaps in the peace of the early morning or in a quiet room after winding down from the day. **This simple rhythm tells your spirit it's time to listen intently.** Have the following materials ready:

◇ Your copy of *By God's Intelligent Design* (the foundation of this study).
◇ This workbook and your Bible (we use the NASB).
◇ A pen or pencil, and a highlighter (don't hesitate to write throughout).

If you find yourself having trouble along the way – whether accessing and downloading the PERSPECTIVES assessments or drafting your design – **please don't hesitate to message us at** <u>ABContrast.com/contact</u>. We're here to help!

Don't hesitate to write in this workbook and in *By God's Intelligent Design*. They are your personal tools for growth, and this process is your personal roadmap. Keep a pen handy to note the words and ideas that provide clues to your design. **Now, it's time to map out your spiritual giftset!**

The Blueprint

Mapping Out Your Divine Design

Welcome to the exciting discovery phase! As you learned in *By God's Intelligent Design*, your spiritual capacity is multi-faceted – often playing out differently in your *thinking*, *socialization*, *leadership*, *following*, *relationships*, and *teamwork*.

To map this unique wiring, we use the **PERSPECTIVES** assessments. If you happen to have existing results, have them ready. If not, you will generate them shortly. First, let's review the foundational elements of your blueprint.

The Foundation: The Four Directions of Preference

First, we start with the foundation – **the core motivations God has wired into you.** Much like a compass, your spirit has a **true north** – a natural direction it wants to travel when you are engaging with the world. You are constantly navigating the tension between **moving fast or slowing down**, and focusing on **the mission** at hand **or the person** in front of you.

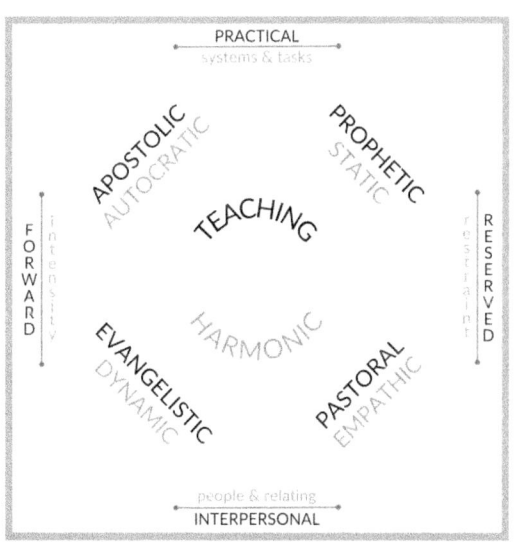

The Four Directions are the foundational **how** (*Pace*) and **why** (*Priority*) behind your choices and actions. They are arranged as two opposing pairs that reveal your natural instincts:

<u>Pace</u> (Forward/Reserved) determines our natural speed of action and reflection.

- ◇ **Forward:** A ministry of **Initiative**. This *Pace* is a drive to act, start new things, and push beyond common obstacles.

- ◇ **Reserved:** A ministry of **Reflection**. This *Pace* instinctively pauses, listens, and observes – to ensure a well-considered path.

<u>Priority</u> (Practical/Interpersonal) determines our primary focus – tasks or people.

◇ **Practical:** A ministry of **Systems**. This *Priority* pursues tasks, tangible goals, structured pathways, and measurable outcomes.

◇ **Interpersonal:** A ministry of **Interaction**. This *Priority* focuses on people, relational exchange, and how everyone can feel included.

Now, let's see how these preferences combine to form five main equipping roles.

The Framing: The Fivefold Equippings

Key combinations of the Four Directions initiate the observable *Pace* and *Priority* behavioral functions of the Five Main Equippings. They are known as the *Fivefold* – not titles to be claimed for prominence, but **capacities to be humbly expressed in service to others**. They are the primary ways God equips His people to build up the church, with each main type playing a vital and indispensable part.

◇ **Apostolic** (Forward *Pace* - Practical *Priority*): *Driving Vision.* The pioneers and architects who accomplish new things and push into new territory.

◇ **Prophetic** (Reserved *Pace* - Practical *Priority*): *Elevating Truth.* The guardians of integrity and composure, who anchor the church in sound doctrine.

◇ **Evangelistic** (Forward *Pace* - Interpersonal *Priority*): *Inspiring Action.* The relational bridges who gather people with an approachable, welcoming spirit.

◇ **Pastoral** (Reserved *Pace* - Interpersonal *Priority*): *Nurturing Care.* The heart of the community, encouraging and shielding with long-term support.

◇ **Teaching** (Centered): *Adding Perspective.* The instructing mediators who can merge the sometimes polarizing *Pace* and *Priority* of the other equipping roles.

These Fivefold roles are more than just names or descriptions; **they are different** *lenses* **through which we see the world and interact with others.** Later, Part 3 explores how these *lenses* lead to both powerful effect and potential misunderstanding – design tensions are framed as *Creative Conflict*.

On the next page, the *pace* and *priority* of your Fivefold wiring comes into focus through your **thinking, speaking, leading, following, relationship,** and **teamwork.**

A 7-Week Study of Spiritual Giftsets and Fivefold Purpose

Your design lives in six distinct *rooms*. It is common, for example, to be an overtly bold Evangelistic gatherer in one room, but a gentle *Pastoral* friend in another. We measure the nuances of your unique **Pace** and **Priority** capacities in:

◇ **Contemplation** and **Connection** (Thinking and Speaking)
◇ **Command** and **Cooperation** (Leading and Following)
◇ **Closeness** (Relationship) and **Contribution** (Teamwork)

It's time to invest 30 minutes to bring your intelligent design into view with a series of free, fun, and fast PERSPECTIVES contrasts – in each of 6 areas! Go to ABContrast.com/perspectives or simply scan this QR code. ▷ ▷ ▷

Optional: the upgrade to **PERSPECTIVES ADVANCED** provides faster flow through, bundled results reports, and bonus content – but the free versions work perfectly for this study.

If you have prior PERSPECTIVES or Premium Content results, feel free to use them.

◇ **Complete All Six Assessments:** Save or print the full 8-page PDF reports, as they are a valuable reference, but **for now you only need the diagram on the first page of each.**

◇ **Record your PERSPECTIVES results: Use this legend ▶** to convert to the **Fivefold Equipping Ministry Matrices**.

 ○ **Each area's result will have (1) one or (2) two main types circled.** If only one ABContrast type is circled, you have an *"unwavering"* alignment there. If two are circled, you have a *"primary-secondary"* scoring.

 ○ **Unwavering and Primary-Secondary examples:**

 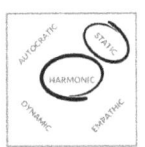

> ABContrast to Fivefold
> Terminology Conversion:
>
> Autocratic = Apostolic
>
> Static = Prophetic
>
> Dynamic = Evangelistic
>
> Empathic = Pastoral
>
> Harmonic = Teaching

 ○ **Your results:** In each area, place a larger circle around your unwavering or primary results – then a smaller circle around any secondary results, if and where applicable.

Contemplation	*Connection*	*Command*	*Cooperation*	*Closeness*	*Contribution*
				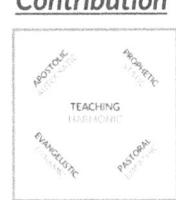	

A Detailed Example: How to Draft Your Design

Before you draft your own PERSPECTIVES results, review this example: After visiting ABContrast.com/perspectives, Charlotte Danner got her results for each area; her process is detailed below and on the following page. The *"page 1"* matrix images from her PERSPECTIVES downloads are shown to the right, with circled ABContrast types (the legend on the next page correlates them to their Fivefold counterparts). *Draft your design with these instructions, and your Fivefold equipping capacities will soon come into focus.*

Contemplation
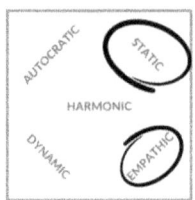

⬦ Step 1 – draft your ***unwavering*** results: Sometimes an area's result indicates a single main type (only one is circled), and preferences are *unwaveringly* aligned. Record these area names near their equipping type, underlined and in ALL CAPS. Observe Charlotte's unwavering alignments appearing in the **CONNECTION** area as Prophetic (*Static* in ABContrast) and in the **CLOSENESS** area as Pastoral (*Empathic* in ABContrast).

Connection

Command
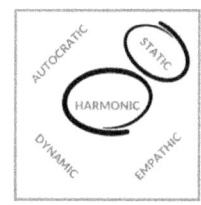

⬦ Step 2 – draft your primary-secondary pairings: When two types are circled, there's a pairing. Write the area name at your primary type, then draw an arrow [→] toward the secondary. Charlotte's **Command** and **Contribution** areas are both primarily Teaching (larger circles at *Harmonic* in ABContrast), with arrows pointing to her identical Prophetic secondary results (smaller circles). ***Pay close attention to the nuances.*** For example, Ms. Danner's **Cooperation** area is primarily Pastoral and secondarily Prophetic (Pastoral → Prophetic). The script flips in **Contemplation**, as it is primarily Prophetic and secondarily Pastoral (Prophetic → Pastoral).

Cooperation

Closeness

Digging Deeper: The Prophetic equipping role is the central theme in Charlotte's design, appearing as either an unwavering, primary, or secondary preference in five of her six areas (all but **Closeness**).

Contribution

Although the four directions aren't shown on this matrix, she is relatively balanced between the *practical* (task) and *interpersonal* (people) priorities. This produces a Teaching capacity, especially in **Command** and **Contribution**. However, due to her strong Prophetic, then Pastoral, alignments (both *reserved*), she will often operate with a distinctly cautious, reflective bias.

Of important note: It's uncharacteristic and draining for Charlotte to exhibit or match the intensity and boldness of a forward-aligned individual. Her Teaching capacity will seem *forward* **only** when interacting with particularly hesitant people. Even then, she shows only a mild to moderate natural assertiveness, and that's limited to the **Contribution** and **Command** areas.

The Six Areas: (EXAMPLE ~ Drafting the Design)

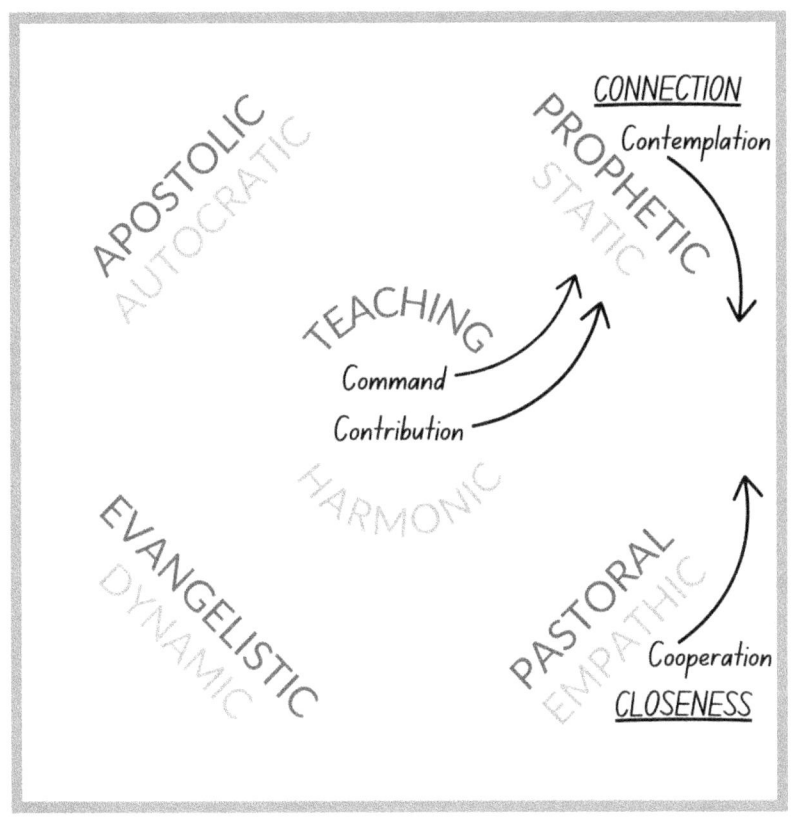

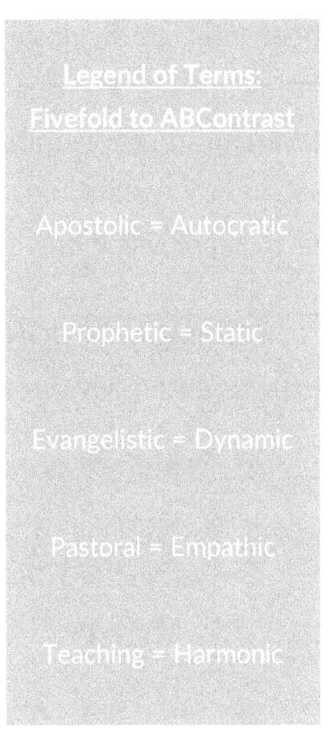

From *By God's Intelligent Design: The Individual's Workbook*, by permission, ©2025 Adam L. Janowski

Name: _Charlotte Danner_   Date: _Feb 29th, 2024_

Thinking/Socializing Equipping(s): _Prophetic → Pastoral; PROPHETIC_

Leading/Following Equipping(s): _Teaching → Prophetic; Pastoral → Prophetic_

Relationship Equipping(s): _PASTORAL_

Teamwork Equipping(s): _Teaching → Prophetic_

<u>*Your Design's Central Theme and Noteworthy Findings*</u>: I have a unique giftset. There's a big Prophetic capacity in my external communications – but also in my thoughts, which are situationally Pastoral. I take charge and team up with a Teaching-Prophetic approach. I engage with relationships through the Pastoral role, and I respond to others' influences there as well. I'll have to be extra intentional to consider the perspectives of people wired in the Forward direction – we're just created differently...

The Six Areas of Your Design:

Using the example and directions on the previous pages, let's see how you've been intelligently designed. Your given capacity is multifaceted. The ABContrast's six areas are our viewing lens for your gifts – **the very tools God intended you to leverage in representing Him to others**. Now, record your unwavering or primary-secondary results in each area on the next page's matrix. (If you need a spare matrix, or to share this with a friend, see page 101.)

COMMUNICATION is how you process your inner world (**Contemplation**) and express externally to others (**Connection**).

◇ **Contemplation (Thinking):** How you think and process internally.
  ❖ My Type(s): _____

◇ **Connection (Speaking):** How you socialize and build rapport.
  ❖ My Type(s): _____

INFLUENCE is your approach to asserting leadership (**Command**) and responding to direction received from others (**Cooperation**).

◇ **Command (Leading):** How you take charge and influence others.
  ❖ My Type(s): _____

◇ **Cooperation (Following):** How you receive and respond to authority.
  ❖ My Type(s): _____

RELATIONSHIP and *TEAMWORK*: Where your combined style of communicated influence plays out in deeper personal bonds (**Closeness**) and within collaborative group settings (**Contribution**).

◇ **Closeness (Relationship):** How you form deep, intimate bonds.
  ❖ My Type(s): _____

◇ **Contribution (Teamwork):** Your natural role in a group effort.
  ❖ My Type(s): _____

A 7-Week Study of Spiritual Giftsets and Fivefold Purpose

See the detailed example on pages 10-11 and draft your area-by-area design here:

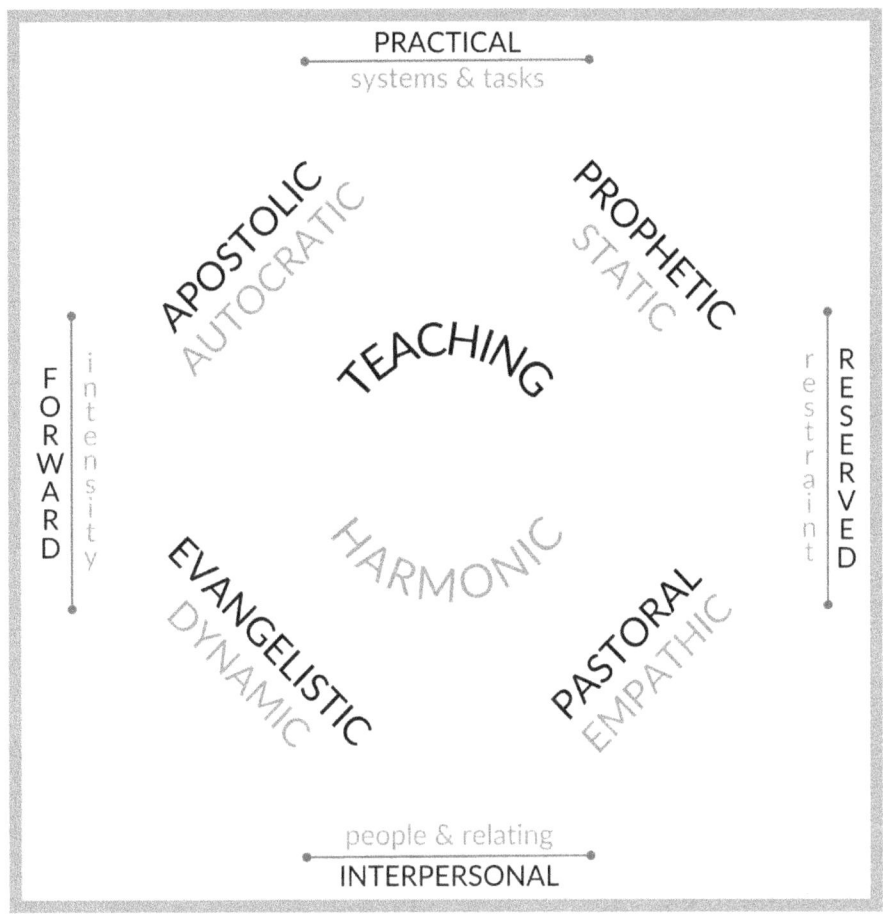

From *By God's Intelligent Design: The Individual's Workbook,* by permission, ©2025 Adam L. Janowski

Name: _____ Date: _____

Thinking/Socializing Equipping(s): _____

Leading/Following Equipping(s): _____

Relationship Equipping(s): _____

Teamwork Equipping(s): _____

Your Design's Central Theme and Noteworthy Findings:

Clues Among Constraints

*Sometimes God reveals our "**Yes**" by giving us a clear "**No**" in our natural wiring. Read these design analogies. Do any of them explain a struggle you've felt?*

For the Pioneer (Apostolic):

◇ Are you restless in comfort? Perhaps you aren't *unmanageable*; perhaps you are an explorer designed to push the boundaries of the "what if," and safety feels like a cage.

◇ Do you have *thick skin*? Perhaps you aren't *unfeeling*; perhaps you are a pioneer designed to push through the thorns of opposition to clear a path for others.

For the Guardian (Prophetic):

◇ Are you sensitive to noise? Perhaps you aren't *distant* or *difficult* so much as you are the tuning fork designed to detect the slightest discord in the church's integrity.

◇ Is your circle of trust small? Maybe you aren't so *unfriendly*; perhaps you are the vault designed to guard the most precious truths.

For the Gatherer (Evangelistic):

◇ Do you have a short attention span for details? Perhaps you aren't *shallow*; maybe your eyes are scanning the horizon for the one person who needs to be included.

◇ Is your voice loud? Perhaps you aren't *obnoxious*; what if you are designed as the trumpet that will rally the crowd in an inspired direction.

For the Nurturer (Pastoral):

◇ Are you risk-averse? Perhaps you aren't *fearful*; maybe you hesitate to jump because your arms are already full of the burdens you diligently carry.

◇ Do you prefer a slow pace? Perhaps you aren't *complacent*; it's likely that you cannot run forward because you refuse to leave the broken behind.

For the Clarifier (Teaching):

◇ Do you get stuck on a single word? Maybe you aren't *obscure*; perhaps you are the microscope designed to reveal the hidden nuances in the text.

◇ Do you struggle to pick a side? Perhaps you aren't indecisive; what if you are the hinge designed to hold two opposing doors open so truth can walk through.

Part 1 is complete – you now hold the blueprint of your design, but a drawing is only the beginning. **The next 7 weeks move you step-by-step through the build site.**

Part 2:

The 7 Weekly Studies for the Individual

Week 1
Your Design's Divine Intent

Project Launch: The Adventure of Discovering Purpose

Every great adventure begins with a single step, and every great structure starts with a cornerstone. This week, we lay that cornerstone by establishing the foundational truth that you have been designed by God for a unique purpose.

The reading in Chapters 1 and 2 of *By God's Intelligent Design* distinguishes between God's universal attributes (His character) and the specific spiritual gifts (His empowerment of our capacity) He entrusts with each of us.

Key Scripture for the Week: *"For we are His workmanship, created in Christ Jesus for good works, which God prepared beforehand, so that we should walk in them."* (Ephesians 2:10)

Week 1: Insights from Your Reading

Now It's time to read through Chapters 1 and 2, then fill in the blanks below to solidify the core concepts. (Use the jumbled letters as a clue for each answer.)

1) Your primary created purpose is: To significantly and meaningfully serve others through your specific and intentionally crafted _____ (**GDESNI**).

2) Our natural abilities and tendencies are our God-given _____ (**AHRDWRAE**). At salvation, the Holy Spirit provides a new _____ (**OAPENRITG STSEYM**) that redeems and reorients our capacity for a Kingdom purpose.

3) A foundational distinction is made between two concepts:

- God's Attributes are _____ (**CARAHECTR**) – who we are all called to become in Christ. This is a universal calling.

- Spiritual Gifts are _____ (**PCATACIY**) – how God most effectively works through your unique design.

Week 1: Personal Reflection

---

4) **Connecting the Dots:** Look back at the sentences you highlighted in Chapters 1 and 2 this week. Choose one phrase that resonated most deeply with you. Write it here and explain why it struck you as significant for your own design.

5) **Your Puzzle Piece Experience:** This week's verse calls us God's *workmanship*. Reflect on a time you felt most like a perfectly fitting *puzzle piece* – energized, effective, and joyful in what you were doing. Also, think of a time when you didn't "fit." Now, analyze those experiences. What specific activities were you engaged in? How did (and didn't) they align with the book's description of serving from the intent of your design? When did it feel like you were operating from your natural *hardware*?

6) **Redeemed Hardware:** The main book explains that spiritual gifts are often our natural, inborn talents redeemed for Kingdom purposes. Think back to your life before you had a mature faith. What were you naturally good at? What activities or roles did you gravitate toward (leading projects, comforting friends, organizing events, etc.)? How do you specifically see God redeeming that same *hardware* for His purposes in your life today?

7) **Attributes vs. Gifts:** The distinction between God's Attributes (like patience) and Spiritual Gifts (like Leadership) is vital. Which of God's attributes do you feel a strong, universal calling to cultivate in your life right now? Take a look through the glossary in Chapter 16 of the main book. Which one or two spiritual gifts elicit a sense of curiosity or resonance in your spirit? Which feel foreign or intimidating? Why do you think that is?

8) **Seeing the Design in Others:** Think of someone you know who serves with a deep sense of joy and effectiveness. How does their role or their way of helping others seem to be a perfect (and natural) fit for their personality? What can you learn from their example of living out their given design?

Week 1: Digging Deeper

1) This study is based on the idea that misunderstanding how we were designed can lead to "friction, burnout, and... miscommunications." In what ways have you seen a *lack of purpose* or a *mismatched role* negatively affect a team or ministry in the past?

2) **Re-read** the section *Your Capacity for Portraying His Character* in Chapter 2 of the main book. What did you feel when reading the example of the **gift** of **Mercy** versus the **attribute** of **mercy**?

3) **Weekly Takeaway:** *My key takeaway this week is that my given purpose is not just about what I do, but about how I reflect... (what comes to mind?)*

Week 1: For Your Exploration This Week

1) **Prayer Focus:** Ask God for clarity on your purpose. Pray, *"Lord, show me how the talents and passions You have already placed in me can best serve others. Open my eyes to the next step of what You have prepared for me."*

2) **Intentionality Surfacing:** Worship is more than singing; it's celebrating the Creator. Exploring your design is an act of worship, as you stand in awe of how *"fearfully and wonderfully made"* you really are (Psalm 139:14). Worship the Architect of your design as you learn and grow this week.

3) **Contemplative Focus:** Find a quiet space and slowly read Psalm 139:13-14: *"For Thou didst form my inward parts; Thou didst weave me in my mother's womb. I will give thanks to Thee, for I am fearfully and wonderfully made; Wonderful are Thy works, And my soul knows it very well."* Instead of analyzing the text, simply pray it back to God. Thank Him for one specific aspect of your **wiring** that you've reflected on this week, even if it's one you sometimes find challenging.

4) **Intelligent Design in Action:** This week, perform two small acts of service. First, do something that feels natural and energizing to you. Second, do something that feels like a stretch or doesn't come as naturally. Reflect on the difference in how you felt performing each task:

5) **Prepare for Next Week:** Before the next lesson, please read Chapters 3 and 4 in *By God's Intelligent Design*.

Week 2
The Fivefold Framework

The Structure: Establishing The Core of Your Unique Design

Key Scripture for the Week: *"And He gave some as apostles, and some as prophets, and some as evangelists, and some as pastors and teachers, for the equipping of the saints for the work of service, to the building up of the body of Christ;"* (Ephesians 4:11-12)

The cornerstone is in place, and it's time to really study the blueprint. This week, we explore the core framework God uses to build His church and see how your design fits the master plan. The reading in Chapters 3 and 4 of *By God's Intelligent Design* introduces the Fivefold Equipping Roles from Ephesians 4 as God's strategic foundation for a healthy church. It also explains the ABContrast model as a real-world lens for identifying how these functions show up in our natural behaviors.

Week 2: Insights from Your Reading

From the reading in Chapters 3 and 4, fill in the blanks below to solidify your understanding of the framework.

1) The expectation for a single leader to fulfill all five roles is an impossible, unbiblical burden that leads to _____ (**BNUORUT**). The Fivefold ministries are God's antidote to this *one-person show* model.

2) Chapter 4 introduces the four directions of preference as *Pace* and *Priority*:

   - ◀ Forward (*Pace*): a ministry of _____ (**IITIIATNVE**).

   - ▶ Reserved (*Pace*): a ministry of _____ (**RFLCEEITON**).

   - ▲ Practical (*Priority*): a ministry of _____ (**SSYMETS**).

   - ▼ Interpersonal (*Priority*): a ministry of _____ (**ITNCAERTION**).

Week 2: Personal Reflection

1) **Connecting the Dots:** Look back at the sentences you highlighted in Chapters 3 and 4 this week. Choose one phrase that resonated most deeply with you. Write it here and explain its personal significance.

2) **Your Blueprint's Story:** Look at your completed matrix from Part 1. What is the big-picture story it tells? Is your design clustered in one quadrant? Is it spread out? Is your public-facing self (Connection, Command) different from your private self (Contemplation, Closeness)? Write down 2-3 initial observations about how you're *wired*. To capture your initial thoughts in even more detail, turn to ***Reflecting on Your Results*** on page 89. Complete the worksheet before moving on. This will be a valuable snapshot to return to – especially at the end of your journey.

3) **Your Main Role:** This week's verse lists the Fivefold equipping roles: Apostolic, Prophetic, Evangelistic, Pastoral, and Teaching. Which of these appears most frequently on your results matrix? Does this align with what you might have guessed, or does it surprise you? Explain your reaction.

4) **The Four Directions in Action:** The four directions of preference (Forward, Reserved, Practical, Interpersonal) show up in our daily choices. Provide a specific example from your past week for each of the following:

   - Did you operate from a Forward (initiating, quick decisions) versus a Reserved (listening, considering carefully) posture? Why and how?

- Was your focus more Practical (tasks, schedules) versus Interpersonal (focus on sentiment and easy warmth)? Why and how?

5) **The Impossible Burden:** The book describes the unfortunate reality that many organizations pressure *a single leader* to fulfill each Fivefold equipping role. Have you ever felt this pressure in a role you've held (leader, parent, or team member)? Open up about how that affected you, and how the Fivefold model offers a healthier alternative:

6) **Seeing the Design in Others:** Observe your family, friends, or a team you're on. Can you identify individuals who naturally lean toward each of the Four Directions? Who is the *Forward* initiator? Who is the *Reserved* observer? Who is the *Practical* organizer? Who is the *Interpersonal* gatherer?

Week 2: Digging Deeper

1) **The book asserts that a healthy church needs all five equipping functions to be active.** Looking honestly at your own church or ministry, which of the five functions do you see most significantly represented? Which underrepresented one seems to be the most needed right now?

2) **Putting it on Paper:** The appendix contains valuable tools to help you synthesize your results. Turn to ***Finalizing Your Fivefold Roles*** on page 87.

Complete the worksheet to clarify your *Foremost*, *Amplifying*, and *Situational* roles. What new insights did this exercise provide you and how does that make you feel?

3) Review the table in Chapter 4 of the main book that maps the five Equipping Roles to their corresponding ABContrast types and Directions of Preference (for example: the Apostolic = Autocratic, and leans Forward-Practical).

4) **Weekly Takeaway:** Complete this sentence: This week, I learned that the diversity of gifts in the church is not a flaw, but is essential for...

Week 2: For Your Exploration This Week

1) **Prayer Focus:** Pray for a spirit of appreciation. *"God, thank you for designing a diverse church. Help me to see the value in those You have wired differently from me. Give me the humility to learn from every part of the body."*

2) **Intentionality Surfacing:** The intentional act of fellowship (Greek: *Koinonia*) is the environment where the Fivefold functions flourish. It's in our shared life together that the pioneer (Apostolic) needs the caregiver (Pastoral), just like the truth-teller (Prophetic) needs the gatherer (Evangelistic). Make time for fellowship in your busy week.

3) **Intelligent Design in Action:** This week, choose one situation where you would normally act according to your dominant preference (such as speaking first if you're Forward). Intentionally choose to act from the opposite preference (like waiting to be the last one to speak). Note what you observed and how it felt.

4) <u>**Prepare for Next Week**</u>: Read Chapters 5 and 6 in *By God's Intelligent Design*.

Week 3
The Practical Priority: Pioneering and Guarding

The Utilities: Understanding the Task-Oriented Equippings

This week, we continue the builder's adventure by taking a deep dive into the framework's **Practical *Priority*** – the task-oriented equippings focused on structure, systems, and measurable outcomes. Your reading in Chapters 5 and 6 of *By God's Intelligent Design* explores the two distinct functions that operate here: the **Apostolic** (*Driving Vision*) and the **Prophetic** (*Elevating Truth*).

Key Scripture for the Week: *"According to the grace of God which was given to me, as a wise master builder I laid a foundation, and another is building upon it. But let each man be careful how he builds upon it."* (1 Corinthians 3:10 and surrounding context)

Note: This week's key scripture offers us a powerful metaphor for the Apostolic role. The Apostle Paul, a quintessential pioneer of the faith, described himself as a **"wise master builder"** who laid a foundation. This offers a picture of a construction expert – perfectly capturing the visionary and task-oriented nature of Apostolic drive. For our study, we will refer to this function as the **Pioneer**, the one who drives vision and breaks new ground for the Kingdom.

The Builder's Briefing: Installing the Utilities

Every construction project relies on essential utilities – the systems that deliver energy, ensure security, and make the structure functional. This week, we are installing the *utilities* of our spiritual design: the Practical, task-oriented functionality.

Your reading in the main book introduced you to two essential workers for this job. The **Apostolic** type is the pioneering tradesman, running new lines, establishing connections, and driving the project forward with visionary utility. The **Prophetic** type is the meticulous manager and inspector, ensuring every feature is up to code and every system is tested in the unchanging standards of truth and integrity.

Both are essential. Without the Apostolic drive, the project never gets off the ground. Without the Prophetic standard, what we build can be risky and unreliable. As you reflect this week, consider how God has wired you to contribute on the practical side of His Kingdom work. Are you called to pioneer what is new, or to guard what is true?

Week 3: Insights from Your Reading

From the reading in Chapters 5 and 6, fill in the blanks below to capture the core concepts of the **Practical** *Priority*, recognizing the unique *Pace* of each equipping.

1) The Apostolic identity is that of a forward-leaning _____ (**NPOIEER**), driven by a need to see big-picture visions come to fruition.

2) The Prophetic function acts as a spiritual _____ (**ACOHNR**), providing the crucial discernment and commitment to standards that guard the integrity of a ministry.

3) Both roles see the **Practical** *Priority*, but they express it differently: the Apostolic capacity builds new _____ (**MYSTSES**) with their **Forward Pace**, while the Prophetic role's **Reserved Pace** ensures existing systems are correct and sound.

Week 3: Personal Reflection

1) **Connecting the Dots:** Look back at the sentences you highlighted in Chapters 5 and 6 this week. Choose one phrase that resonated most deeply with you. Write it here and explain why you feel it stood out.

2) **Your Inner Pioneer (Apostolic):** This week's key scripture describes the Apostle Paul using the metaphor of a *"wise master builder."* This is the heart of

Apostolic drive – a pioneering and advancing force. When, how, and where does this pioneering energy show up in your life? Describe a time when you felt a strong urge to implement a solution, start a new project, draft a strategic plan, build something, or organize a complex event. What about that process felt energizing?

3) **Your Inner Guardian (Prophetic):** Chapter 6 frames the Prophetic function as the *guardian of spiritual integrity*. Where do you feel a deep, personal need for things to be right, true, fair, and principled? Think of a time when you felt compelled to *speak up for the standard* or ask clarifying questions to ensure a plan was sound, even when it might have slowed things down. What principle were you defending?

4) **Pioneering vs. Guarding:** Imagine you are part of a team planning a major ministry event. Do you see yourself more as the visionary architect sketching the bold new plan (Apostolic)? Or as the meticulous inspector ensuring every detail aligns with the mission and budget (Prophetic)? Explain your choice with a real-life example.

5) **The Practical priority in Your Life:** Look at your completed Intelligent Design Matrix. Where do the Practical equippings (Apostolic or Prophetic) show up most deeply in your six areas? For example, is your Command (leadership) style more Apostolic (vision-casting), while your Cooperation (follower) style is more Prophetic (ensuring standards are met)? **How does this resonate with your real-life experiences?**

6) **Personal Dialogue:** How do these two *voices* show up in your thought life and decision-making? Think about a recent important decision. Which part of you was the *Apostolic* thinking, pushing for action and a new future? Which part was the *Prophetic* thought, urging caution and adherence to your principles? How did you navigate that private thought process?

7) **Seeing the Design in Others:** Think of two people you know fairly well: one who is a great project-starter and visionary (Apostolic) and another who is a meticulous fact-checker and standard-keeper (Prophetic). How do their practical strengths differ but complement each other? How have you benefited from both types of people in your life?

8) **Be a Design Detective:** This week, your task is to be an observer of God's design in those you know rather well. In a meeting, family conversation, or team project, watch for the Practical perspective in action. Without judging, simply note one example of someone operating in a pioneering, *let's build it* way (Apostolic) and one example of someone operating in a principled, *let's get it right* way (Prophetic). What was the outcome of their effort and approach?

Week 3: Digging Deeper

1) **The Apostolic wants to move fast and build, while the Prophetic wants to ensure everything is correct.** How can a team foster a culture where the Prophetic *guardian* voice is seen as a valuable partner, rather than just a roadblock?

2) **Re-read the section on Nehemiah in Chapter 5 of the main book.** Reflect on how he balanced a Practical survey of the broken walls with a Forward call to action to rebuild them.

3) **Weekly Takeaway:** Complete the following sentence: This week, I saw my own *Practical* side show up when I...

Week 3: For Your Exploration This Week

1) **Prayer Focus:** Pray for the wisdom to know when to pioneer new things and when to define and guard what is true and established. Ask God to show you which mode – pioneering or guarding – is most needed in your life this week.

2) **Intentionality Surfacing:** Study is essential for the Practical function. The Apostolic pioneer must review the landscape before building, and the Prophetic guardian must know the standards (like scripture) to protect them faithfully. Consider these principles as you encounter all this week has to offer.

3) **Intelligent Design in Action:** This week, apply each *Pace* of the Practical axis. First, build something by drafting a simple, one-page plan for a personal goal you want to accomplish (**Forward Pace**). Second, guard something by meticulously proofreading an important email, message, or document before you send it (**Reserved Pace**).

4) **Prepare for Next Week:** Before our next session, please read Chapters 7 and 8 in *By God's Intelligent Design*.

Week 4
The Interpersonal Priority: Gathering and Caring

The Finishes: Understanding the People-Oriented Equippings

Key Scripture for the Week: *"So then, while we have opportunity, let us do good to all men, and especially to those who are of the household of the faith."* (Galatians 6:10)

What you've been building should also feel welcoming, right? This week, we shift to the other side of the matrix to explore the finishes – the **Interpersonal** *Priority*, which focuses on people, relationships, and a warm sense of community. Your reading in Chapters 7 and 8 of the main book will introduce you to the Evangelistic (*Inspiring Action*) and Pastoral (*Nurturing Care*) functions.

The Builder's Briefing: Applying the Finishes

A structure isn't a home until the finishes are applied – **the elements that make it warm, welcoming, and a place where people want to be.** This week, we shift our focus to the Interpersonal, people-oriented prioritizations, the *"finishes"* that transform a functional building into a thriving community.

You've just read about the two artisans responsible for this important work. The **Evangelistic** operates as the designer of the grand, welcoming entryway, inspiring action and producing an atmosphere of excitement that draws people in from the outside. The **Pastoral** curates the comfortable, safe living room, nurturing the existing community with long-term care and ensuring everyone inside feels protected and valued. **A house needs both a front door and a living room to be a home.**

As you work through this week's questions, think about your relational instincts. Are you energized by gathering new people, or by caring for those already present?

Week 4: Insights from Your Reading

As you read Chapters 7 and 8, fill in the blanks to solidify your understanding of the **Interpersonal** *Priority*, recognizing the unique *Pace* of each equipping.

1) The heart of the Evangelistic role is using approachable energy and a passion for people to inspire _____ (**TICAON**), break down barriers, and foster a warm environment.

2) Both roles are people-focused, but with different energy: the Evangelistic capacity focuses on _____ (**TRAGHENIG**) new people in, while the Pastoral nature excels at caring for the existing flock.

3) The main book uses the example of Barnabas, whose name means "*son of _____ (ENEEMOUGRACNT*)," to model the Pastoral function's **Interpersonal** *Priority* (**Reserved** *Pace*) of advocating for and restoring others. In contrast, there are several New Testament accounts of Peter's Evangelistic tendencies (**Interpersonal** *Priority*, **Forward** *Pace*) on overt display.

Week 4: Personal Reflection

1) **Connecting the Dots:** Look back at the sentences you highlighted in Chapters 7 and 8 this week. Choose one phrase that resonated most deeply with you. Write it here and explain the personal significance.

2) **Your Inner Gatherer (Evangelistic):** Chapter 7 describes the Evangelistic strength as a *relational bridge*. Think about times you've been excited to share something – good news, a favorite restaurant, an uplifting story, or your faith. What motivates you to excitedly share? Do you feel energized by bringing new people into an experience or community? Describe a time you acted as that "bridge" to inspired action and gathering people to yourself.

3) **Your Inner Nurturer (Pastoral):** Chapter 8 frames the Pastoral type as the *heart of community*. Who are the people in your life that you feel a natural, long-term responsibility to care for and shield from hardship? Think of a time you walked alongside someone through a difficult season – not with a quick fix, but through steady presence, listening, and quiet acts of service. What did that experience feel like for you?

4) **Applying the Finishes – Gathering vs. Caring:** Which role feels more natural to you: acting as the host who throws open the doors for a grand housewarming party, making a high-energy, welcoming atmosphere for many new guests (Evangelistic)? Or curating a quiet, comfortable room where a few close friends can feel safe enough for deep, vulnerable conversation (Pastoral)? Explain:

5) **Bubbly vs. Nurturing:** The Evangelistic individual is energized by gathering new people, while the Pastoral person focuses on caring for those already present. Describe a time you have felt this *gathering vs. caring* tension in your own heart or ministry. How did you, or how could you, navigate that tension to honor both impulses?

6) **The Interpersonal *Priority* in Your Life:** Look at your completed Intelligent Design Matrix. How are the Interpersonal equippings expressed in your design? For example, might your Connection (socializing) style be more Evangelistic (*high-energy, gathering*), while your Closeness style (deep bonds) is more Pastoral (*nurturing, quiet care*)? How does warm approachability enter your interactions?

7) **Seeing the Design in Others:** Think of one person who is a natural *gatherer* and another who is clearly a *nurturer*. How do they show they care for people in different but equally valuable ways? What can you learn from their examples about the extent of God's love?

Week 4: A Case Study in Contrasting Perspectives

Read the story of the sharp disagreement in Acts 15:37-39 over John Mark. Paul, operating in an **Apostolic** manner (*Forward-Practical*), was focused on the urgency and security of the mission. Barnabas, operating in a **Pastoral** manner (*Reserved-Interpersonal*), was focused on the restoration of the person, John Mark.

1) From your primary *Pace* and *Priority* perspective, whose side do you naturally sympathize with? Why?

2) Often, we view an opposing perspective as "wrong," yet both men had valid points. What was the risk to the early church if they had only followed Paul's instinct? Conversely, what might have been conceded if they only followed Barnabas?

3) How does understanding their specific design wiring help you view this not as a "fight," but as two necessary priorities in temporary tension?

Week 4: Digging Deeper

1) **Ministries often struggle with the tension between being *outward-focused* (Evangelistic) and *inward-focused* (Pastoral).** How can a church ensure its passion for reaching new people doesn't come at the expense of caring for the existing flock, and vice versa?

2) **Re-read the section on Barnabas in Chapter 8 of the main book.** His name means "*son of encouragement,*" and he perfectly modeled the Pastoral function of advocating for and restoring others. Your thoughts?

3) **Weekly Takeaway:** Complete the following sentence: "*This past week, I was challenged to balance my focus between reaching out to new people and...*"

Week 4: For Your Exploration This Week

1) **Prayer Focus:** Ask God for a heart that reflects His love for both those outside the community and those within it. Pray, "*Lord, show me one person this week I can invite in, and one person I can care for.*"

2) **Intentionality Applied:** Hospitality is central to the **Interpersonal *Priority***. It is practiced by the Evangelistic person who presents a welcoming ***front door*** for newcomers and by the Pastoral individual who offers a safe, ***caring space*** for the existing flock.

3) **Intelligent Design in Action:** This week, put each ***Pace*** of the Interpersonal axis into practice. First, perform a gathering action by reaching out to someone

new or inviting someone to join an activity (**Forward** *Pace*). Second, perform a caring action by checking in on a friend or family member who you know is going through a difficult season (**Reserved** *Pace*).

4) **Prepare for Next Week:** Before our next session, please read Chapters 9 and 10 in *By God's Intelligent Design*.

Week 5
The Mediating Equipping and Our Shadow Sides

The Inspection: Embracing Strengths and Struggles with Grace

Every builder knows that a thorough inspection is essential for a structure's integrity, and every explorer must learn to read the terrain. This week, we conduct a vital inspection of our design, exploring the balanced, mediating Teaching role and a key concept for our journey: the *Shadow Side*. **This is a courageous look at both the strengths that propel us forward and the struggles we must navigate with grace.**

Your reading in Chapters 9 and 10 of By God's Intelligent Design will provide the clarity needed for this week's honest reflection.

Key Scripture for the Week: *"But let each one examine his own work, and then he will have reason for boasting in regard to himself alone, and not in regard to another."* (Galatians 6:4)

The Builder's Briefing: Checks, Balances, and Adjustments

Before any project is complete, a builder is subjected to a thorough inspection, walking through the site to draft a *punch list* of items that need adjustment. **This week is our official inspection.** It requires an honest look at how all the systems work together and the courage to identify potential flaws – not for condemnation, but for completion. Your reading introduced you to the two key aspects of this inspection.

First is **Teaching**, the inspector whose viewpoint comes from understanding how Apostolic energy distribution, Prophetic managing, Evangelistic design, and Pastoral comfort each are meant to integrate into a cohesive whole.

Second is the concept of the *Shadow Side,* our willingness to inspect for the hidden structural weaknesses or code violations in our own design that could compromise the integrity of our work if left unaddressed. This inspection is the path to maturity. As you reflect, ask God for the Teaching capacity's clarity and the accompanying humility of a wise builder.

Week 5: Insights from Your Reading

As you read Chapters 9 and 10, fill in the blanks below to understand the balance between our strengths and struggles.

1) The Teaching type is a grounded _____ (**RCLAFIIER**), who ensures others will learn, grow, and be protected from directional doctrine that is too singularly focused.

2) The *Shadow Side* occurs when a spiritual ability becomes a counterproductive energy because it's exercised without _____ (**AMYTIRUT**), _____ (**EVLO**), or _____ (**ACCTILIBATNUOY**).

3) The five *shadows* are:

   - Apostolic → **Driven** _____ (**DROTATCI**)

   - Prophetic → **Harsh** _____ (**JEGDU**)

   - Evangelistic → **Performing** _____ (**PESAELR**)

   - Pastoral → **Appeasing** _____ (**ENLBARE**)

   - Teaching → **Proud** _____ (**ETSIILT**)

Week 5: Personal Reflection

1) **Connecting the Dots:** Look back at the sentences you highlighted in Chapters 9 and 10 this week. Choose one phrase that resonated most deeply with you. Write it here and explain why it was so impactful.

2) **Your Inner Mediator (Teaching):** Chapter 9 describes the Teaching type as a *grounded clarifier* who connects different viewpoints. Think of a time you found yourself explaining a complex idea, helping two people in a disagreement see each other's point of view, or bringing a balanced perspective to a heated conversation. What about that role felt natural or fulfilling? How were you *adding perspective* to the situation?

3) **Confronting Your *Shadow Side*:** Prayerfully read the five *Shadow Side* descriptions in Chapter 10 with open mindedness rather than through a lens of judgment. Simply ask God, *"Where in my life do these tendencies show up, and how can I better conform to Your will for me in that moment?"* Reflect on which description feels most familiar, especially as it seems to show up when you're under stress, feeling insecure, or even operating in an undeveloped facet of spiritual maturity. **Remember, these are tendencies, not identities.**

4) **Prudent Building:** A wise builder conducts a thorough inspection (self-scrutiny) before others get a chance. As you inspect your own design, which *Shadow Side* tendency from Chapter 10 have you placed under self-control? Describe a situation where this *code violation* emerged under pressure.

5) **The Path to Wholeness:** Chapter 10 outlines a three-fold remedy to the *Shadow Side*: Willing Self-Awareness (looking **INWARD**), Deep Accountability (looking **OUTWARD**), and the Fruit of the Spirit (looking **UPWARD**). As you consider the *shadow* you just identified, which of these three remedies do you feel is most needed in your life right now? What is one small, practical step you could take this week to pursue it?

6) **Your Inner World:** The Contemplation (thinking) area is where our strengths and *shadows* often first emerge. Look at your result for this area on your matrix. How does your primary equipping role shape your thought life? For example, does an Apostolic thinker constantly strategize, while a Pastoral thinker continually reflects on people's well-being? How has your *Shadow Side* first appeared in your thoughts before it became a spoken word or action?

7) **Draft a Growth Plan:** It's time to apply these insights with ***Navigating My Shadow Side*** on page 95. Complete the worksheet to form your personal plan for grace and growth. The most convicting thing I learned about my *Shadow Side* this week is...

8) **Seeing the Design in Others:** Think of someone you consider great at teaching (in any area of life). What makes them so effective at helping others understand? Now, reflect on a time you saw a *Shadow Side* – in yourself or someone else – emerge under stress. How did (or could) grace and understanding help that situation?

Week 5: Digging Deeper

1) **The *Shadow Side* emerges most often when the worries of this world dominate our thoughts.** What are the common stressors that tend to push you outside of a healthy expression of your giftset?

2) **Re-read the table** *Kingdom-Minded Pathway* **in the main book, on page 114 of Chapter 10.** For the *shadow* you identified with most, focus on the corresponding pathway (for example, for the *Harsh Judge*, the pathway is "Speaking The Truth In Love With Tact").

3) **Weekly Takeaway: Complete this sentence:** The most convicting thing I learned about my *Shadow Side* this week is... **(and explain why)**

Week 5: For Your Journey This Week

1) **Prayer Focus:** Pray for humility and courage. *"God, give me the courage to see my own Shadow Side clearly and without shame. Help me to have grace for others when their struggles surface, just as You do for me."*

2) **Intentionality Surfacing:** Confession is a powerful antidote to our **Shadow Side**. It brings what is hidden into the light, inviting God's grace and the support of trusted accountability partners to bring healing and freedom. This week, remain open to when you can leverage a humble, open admission to free yourself from old burdens by way of new grace through accountability.

3) **Intelligent Design in Action:** This week, practice the healthy expression of the Teaching function by explaining a concept you understand well to someone else who doesn't, focusing entirely on their understanding. Then, identify one situation or "trigger" that tends to bring out your **Proud Elitist** *Shadow Side*.

4) **Prepare for Next Week:** Before our next session, please read Chapters 11 and 12 in *By God's Intelligent Design*.

Week 6
Kingdom-Minded Collaboration

The Walkthrough: Function, Feel, and Systems Checks

Key Scripture: *"from whom the whole body, being fitted and held together by that which every joint supplies, according to the proper working of each individual part, causes the growth of the body for the building up of itself in love."* (Ephesians 4:16)

With the structure built and inspected, we go on the walkthrough. **We move from understanding the design to applying your design in the real world, preparing you for the continuing journey ahead.** The reading in Chapters 11 and 12 of the main book is key for this crucial step.

The Builder's Briefing: The Workshop

With the blueprint understood and the structure inspected, it's time to enter the workshop. **A design is only as good as the builder's ability to use their tools, and this week is about moving from theory to practice.** It's about learning to steward the tools God has given you with skill, wisdom, and purpose.

Your reading this week focused on the craftsman's core process: **the Discern, Develop, and Deploy cycle.** This is how we identify the right tool for the job (**Discern**), learn to handle it with skill (**Develop**), and use it to build something beautiful (**Deploy**).

You also learned that the *Creative Conflict* that arises when different builders work together isn't a problem; it's the very friction that sharpens our tools and refines our work. As you engage with the questions this week, think of yourself as an apprentice in God's workshop, **ready to hone your craft for the Master Builder**.

Week 6: Insights from Your Reading

As you read Chapters 11 and 12, fill in the blanks below to grasp these key application principles.

1) True stewardship is a three-part cycle: _____ **(DICSNRE)** (awareness), _____ **(DVEPOLE)** (preparation), and _____ **(DYOLPE)** (willingness).

2) We are called to be proactive _____ **(TTAEHSMORTS)** that set a spiritual temperature, not passive _____ **(SREMOTEMREHT)** that merely reflect it.

3) The pressure between accessibility and truth, or relationship and principle, is between the _____ **(GELISTIVACEN)** and _____ **(PRHETIOPC)** equippings.

4) The conflict between _____ **(APOSTLICO)** and _____ **(PATORSAL)** is the classic tension between task and people, or mission and community.

Week 6: Personal Reflection

1) **Connecting the Dots:** Look back at the sentences you highlighted in Chapters 11 and 12 this week. Choose one phrase that resonated most deeply with you. Write about why it's important to your growth trajectory.

2) **Your Place in the Cycle:** This week's verse calls us to be *"good stewards."* With that in mind, consider the Discern, Develop, Deploy cycle from Chapter 11. As you think about the primary spiritual function suggested by your matrix, where do you see yourself right now? Are you still trying to discern them? Are you actively developing them? Or are you

confidently deploying them? What's one specific step you can take this month to move forward in that process?

3) **Tool Inspection:** As you look again at your completed matrix, what is the most familiar tool in your workshop (your biggest confirmation)? What tool did you discover that you didn't know you had (your biggest surprise)?

4) **Personal Tensions:** Where do you see significant *creative conflict* within even your own design? For example, is your Connection style more distant and serious, but your Closeness style is warm and bubbly? How does that unfold in real life?

5) **Thermostat or Thermometer?:** Reflect on a real-life situation from the past month where you acted like a *thermometer* – passively reflecting the stress or negativity of the environment. Based on your design, how could you have improved the atmosphere as a *thermostat* instead – proactively introducing peace, clarity, or inspiration?

6) **Your Role in Conflict:** Chapter 12 details two common conflicts: Apostolic/Pastoral (task vs. people) and Evangelistic/Prophetic (accessibility vs. truth). Which of these two tensions do you find yourself in most often? How does reframing it as *an organically-occurring, necessary feature*, rather than a problem, change how you might approach it in the future?

7) **Collaborate with a Plan**: To better understand how to navigate contrasting biases, turn to ***From Creative Conflict to Collaboration*** on page 91. Complete Part 1 by mapping out a key group in your life (family, work team, ministry, etc.). What does this exercise reveal about your group's collective strengths and blind spots? Can you identify a recent example where different equippings were at odds but that initial friction ultimately led to a better outcome? How did balancing the diverse perspectives enhance the result?

Week 6: Digging Deeper

1) Re-read the section *The Thermometer Becomes a Thermostat* in Chapter 11 of the main book. What is one practical way you can move from being a reactive "thermometer" to a proactive "thermostat" this very week?

2) **Intelligent Design in Action**: Suppose a team meeting has become negative and critical. A thermometer would reflect the negativity. A thermostat would change the temperature. Based on YOUR primary equipping, what is one specific thermostat action you could take? (For example, an Apostolic type might say, "Let's refocus on the vision," a Pastoral type may offer, "It sounds like people are feeling discouraged. Can we talk about that?"; or a Teaching type could say: "Let's step back and look at the facts from a different angle.")

3) Consider a specific environment (your workplace, home, a committee) where God might be calling you to begin functioning as an atmosphere-altering thermostat? What would that adjustment look like?

4) **Weekly Takeaway:** Scenario – envision that you succeeded in the items above. Complete this sentence: The most important step I took to be a *thermostat* instead of a *thermometer* was to...

Week 6: For Your Exploration This Week

1) **Prayer Focus:** Pray for courage and opportunity. "*Lord, give me the courage to be a Kingdom-minded thermostat. Show me one specific opportunity this week to deploy these abilities to serve someone else.*"

2) **Intentionality Surfacing:** Service is the essence of design stewardship. It is the practice of moving beyond simply knowing our giftsets to actively and humbly using them for the good of others, without needing recognition. Make the time to actively serve someone this week – not for praise or to accomplish your agenda, but quietly without any *strings attached*.

3) **Prepare for Next Week:** Before our final session, please read Chapters 13 and 14 in *By God's Intelligent Design*.

4) **Linking Roles to Gifts:** This is where your blueprint becomes a detailed action plan. Turn to ***Linking Your Design to Specific Gifts*** on page 99. Use your matrix results and the glossary in Chapter 16 of the main book to complete the worksheet. Which 2-3 specific gifts (Administration, Hospitality, Mercy,

etc.) align most deeply with your design? Write down those gifts and explain why you believe they connect to your results.

◇ Gift:

    o Notes:

◇ Gift:

    o Notes:

◇ Gift:

    o Notes:

Week 7
Deploying Your
Design Intelligently

The Keys: Stewardship for Impact and Investment Returns

The build is complete; the structure is sound. Take hold of the keys, and bring all the concepts of your builder's adventure together to unlock a lifetime of faithful investment. It's time to deploy the tools of your unique design.

Don't forget the insights from Chapters 13 and 14 as you humbly engage in service to others. Now we'll leverage the *Glossary of Spiritual Gifts* in Chapter 16 as a tool to further define your Kingdom attributes.

Key Scripture for the Week: *"Whatever you do, do your work heartily, as for the Lord rather than for men; knowing that from the Lord you will receive the reward of the inheritance. It is the Lord Christ whom you serve."* (Colossians 3:23-24)

The Builder's Briefing: Taking Ownership with the Keys

With the construction complete, and the tools secured, **this final week is about taking ownership of the finished work and shifting focus to investment returns.** The blueprint has served its purpose; now, you hold the keys to unlock doors of opportunity for Kingdom impact.

Your reading in the final chapters of the main book was a charge to action – a call to move from understanding your design to applying it with love and humility in a world of diverse people. **This is the heart of stewardship.** The goal was never just to build, but to establish a base for a grander adventure. The reflection questions this week are your keys to stewardship, designed to help you **maximize the *Kingdom Yield* (ROI)** as you step out in faith, ready to live out your purpose.

Week 7: Insights from Your Reading

As you read Chapters 13 and 14, fill in the blanks below.

1) Chapter 13 teaches that healthy ministry teams are intentionally built for _____ (**LAABNCE**), not for the comfort of similarity.

2) By intelligent design, a wise leader matches people to roles based on their God-given _____ (**GTITFSE**) and behavioral style, which prevents burnout, increases effect, and cultivates joy.

3) As 1 Corinthians 13 makes clear, _____ (**EOVL**) is the indispensable context for all spiritual gifts, without which even the most spectacular endowments are rendered hollow and spiritually ineffective.

Week 7: Personal Reflection

1) **Connecting the Dots:** Look back at the sentences you highlighted in Chapters 13 and 14 this week. Choose one phrase that resonated most deeply with you. Write it here and explain how you'll apply it going forward.

2) **Your Personal Blueprint:** This week's verse calls us to do our work *"heartily."* Look back at the *Linking Your Design to Specific Gifts* worksheet you completed for homework. What is the single biggest confirmation – a specific gift you already knew God had designed in you?

3) **Seeing the Design in Others:** Think about a team you are on (your family, a small group, or a work team). Looking at the Fivefold model, which gifts seem to be robustly represented in the group? Which ones might be less present? How does this affect the overall enthusiasm and effectiveness?

Kingdom Economics: The Investment Yield Menu

Now that you've identified your specific gifts, let's look at how to invest them for a return. In Mark 4, Jesus describes seed that falls on good soil, producing a crop that yields "thirty, sixty, and a hundredfold." When we apply our design, we aren't just *being productive* – we are generating a return on God's investment in us.

- **30x (Personal Habits):** This is where you master your design in private so it can be trusted in public. It is faithfulness in the small things.

- **60x (Relational Impact):** Start to bless your immediate circle through your design – your family, small group, or team. It's moving from *sitting* to *serving*.

- **100x (Cultural Shift):** This is when your design creates a legacy level representation of God's goodness – a system or culture with the potential to affect even the people you may never meet.

Instructions: Use the *Kingdom ROI* menus on the following pages to brainstorm where you might fulfill your **30x, 60x, or 100x Yield**. Consider all six areas – **thinking** (Contemplation), **socialization** (Connection), **leading** (Command), **following** (Cooperation), **relationship** (Closeness), and **teamwork** (Contribution). Certain teams or roles will spark your interest, even if the position's specific function in a ministry or at your church is different – select them with a circle or underline.

Kingdom ROI via the APOSTOLIC (Pioneer)

◈ **30x Yield** (The Daily Habit): *The Initiator.* Be the one in your family or workplace who spots a lingering problem and proposes the first step to fix it. Don't just join the masses in stating what **could be**... build a real solution.

◈ **60x Yield** (The Ministry Role): *Initiative Building*

  o *Best Fits:* Church Plant Team, Strategic Planning Committee, Outreach Coordination, Capital Campaign Team, Leadership Development.

  o *Why:* You need roles where you can start new things, solve structural problems, or drive things onward. You thrive if there is a hill to take or a problem to solve.

◈ **100x Yield** (The Kingdom Venture): *The Entrepreneur.* Organize a neighborhood dinner, launch a faith-based business, or assemble a city-wide prayer march.

Kingdom ROI via the PROPHETIC (Guardian)

◈ **30x Yield** (The Daily Habit): *The Truth-Speaker.* In your close relationships, be the one who gently asks the hard question that leads to a breakthrough. Speak identity into your peers, friends, children, or spouse.

◈ **60x Yield** (The Ministry Role): *Oversight Applications*

  o *Best Fits:* Finance/Budget Committee (Ensuring Integrity), Safety and Security Team, Curriculum Review, Intercessory Prayer Team, Tech/Production (Systems and Excellence).

  o *Why:* You need roles where you can guard the integrity of the ministry, ensure standards are met, or discern spiritual direction. You thrive where details, accuracy, and truth matter.

◈ **100x Yield** (The Kingdom Venture): *The Advocate.* Join a school board to advocate for values, serve on a board of ethics, or write to influence culture with biblical truth.

Kingdom ROI via the EVANGELISTIC (Gatherer)

◈ **30x Yield** (The Daily Habit): *The Inviter.* Commit to learning the name of your barista, mail carrier, or gym partner. Be the bridge that connects your neighbors to one another.

◈ **60x Yield** (The Ministry Role): *Front-Facing Teams*

- o *Best Fits:* Greeters/Parking Team (First Impressions), Coffee/Hospitality, Social Media/Marketing, Youth Ministry (Games/Energy), Special Events Team.

- o *Why:* You need roles that are outward-facing, high-energy, and allow you to break the ice with strangers. You thrive where the goal is to make people feel welcome and excited.

- ◈ **100x Yield** (The Kingdom Venture): *The Community Builder.* Host a neighborhood block party, run a community sports league, or lead a workplace morale initiative.

Kingdom ROI via the PASTORAL (Nurturer)

- ◈ **30x Yield** (The Daily Habit): *The Listener.* Be the safe harbor for a friend in crisis. Send a text of specific support to a different person every morning.

- ◈ **60x Yield** (The Ministry Role): *Shepherding Teams*

  - o *Best Fits:* Small Group Co-Leader, Care Ministry (Meal Trains, Hospital Visits), Nursery/Preschool (Nurturing), Recovery Group Facilitator, New Believer Follow-Up.

  - o *Why:* You need roles that allow for long-term connection, restorative shepherding, and secure, one-on-one care. You thrive where you can sit with people and ensure they feel seen and protected.

- ◈ **100x Yield** (The Kingdom Venture): *The Refuge.* Become a foster parent, start a support group for grief or addiction in your city, or mentor at-risk youth.

Kingdom ROI via TEACHING (Clarifier)

- ◈ **30x Yield** (The Daily Habit): *The Mentor.* When someone less informed is confused, use your giftset to explain the "why" behind the "what" with patience and clarity. Bring calm to chaos.

- ◈ **60x Yield** (The Ministry Role): *Instruction and Discipleship*

  - o *Best Fits:* Bible Study Teacher, Small Group Curriculum Writer, Discipleship Mentor, Next Steps/Class Instructor, Mediation/Conflict Resolution Team.

  - o *Why:* You need roles where you can bring clarity to confusion, explain deep truths simply, or help balance differing viewpoints. You thrive where understanding and growth are the goals.

- ◈ **100x Yield** (The Kingdom Venture): *The Thought Leader.* Write a blog, lead a community book club, or teach a life-skills class at a local shelter.

Stewardship for the ROI Challenge

Your challenge: It's time to move from insight to intentional action. **God gave you a unique design capacity as a spiritual capital investment.** From the perspective of your primary role, brainstorm what faithfulness looks like at three levels of return.

Step 1: Verify Your Assets and Risk

◇ **My Foremost Equipping Role:** _____

(Teaching, Pastoral, Evangelistic, Prophetic, and/or Apostolic)

◇ **My Associated Gifts:** _____

(for example, gifts such as Administration, Hospitality, Writing, Mercy, and Wisdom)

◇ **My Primary *Shadow* (Risk):** _____

(Appeasing Enabler, Driven Dictator, Proud Elitist, Harsh Judge, or Performing Pleaser)

Step 2: The 30x Yield (The Daily Habit)

Focus: Personal Growth, Communication, Close Relationships, Healthy Boundaries.

◇ **The Goal:** I'll use my gift of [*insert gift name*] to improve my daily interactions by [*...insert action...*]. **Pastoral Example:** *"I'll use my gift of Mercy to listen without fixing when my spouse vents."* **Prophetic Example:** *"I'll use my gift of Wisdom to pause for 30 seconds before offering a critique."*

◇ **My 30x Action, with the barriers and breakthroughs along the way:**

Step 3: The 60x Yield (The Ministry Role)

Focus: Meeting Needs Regularly, Frequent Ministry Service, Concrete Action Steps.

◇ **The Goal:** I can apply my unique wiring to fill a specific need in the body by [*...insert action...*]. **Apostolic Example:** *"I can offer to lead the launch team for the* *new youth initiative."* **Teaching Example:** *"I can volunteer to mentor a new believer using my balanced clarity and mediating perspective."*

◈ **My 60x Action, with the barriers and breakthroughs along the way:**

Step 4: The 100x Yield (The Kingdom Venture)

◈ **The Goal:** I could step out in faith to impact the world around me by [*...insert action...*]. **Evangelistic Example:** *"I could host a neighborhood block party to connect with the unchurched."* **Prophetic Example:** *"I could join a local school board committee to advocate for integrity."*

◈ **My 100x Action, with the barriers and breakthroughs along the way:**

Step 5: The Commitment

For the next 30 days, **I will not just bury my talent; I will put it to work.** I commit before God to investing my spiritual giftset (*Kingdom capacities*) through:

Signature: _____ Date: _____

Don't rely on memory alone – record your *Breakthroughs* (what was easy) and your *Barriers* (what wasn't) on the very next page.

My Harvest Log

Make a record of your intentional efforts as follows:

Date: _____   Circle One: **30x** *or* **60x** *or* **100x**

Breakthrough *(the WIN)*: _____

Barrier *(the OBSTACLE)*: _____

Other Notes: _____

Date: _____   Circle One: **30x** *or* **60x** *or* **100x**

Breakthrough *(the WIN)*: _____

Barrier *(the OBSTACLE)*: _____

Other Notes: _____

Week 7: For Your Exploration This Week

1) **Prayer Focus:** Pray a prayer of commissioning. *"Lord, thank You for choosing to make me this way. I accept this design as a good gift from You. Provide me the courage and joy to walk boldly and humbly in the purpose You have for me."*

2) **Congratulations:** You've completed the individual's 7-week core study! Take the *Investment Yield Challenge* to heart over the next month, putting your design into action by **moving from insight to impact**. This is where real growth happens, and we've included **a Bonus Week 8 session** to serve as your accountability check-in. **Once you have successfully completed your 30-Day challenge,** continue with **Week 8** to reflect on your experiences and celebrate your progress.

(Bonus) Week 8
Living Out Your Design

The Continuation: From Discovery to Discipleship

Key Scripture for the Week: *"And let us not lose heart in doing good, for in due time we shall reap if we do not grow weary."* (Galatians 6:9)

This session is designed to be used upon completion of your **Investment Yield Challenge** – to move from the initial discovery to the ongoing adventure of stewardship. **This is a time to reflect on your real-world experiences, troubleshoot obstacles, and celebrate the ongoing journey of living out your intelligent design.** The only preparation for this session is to have completed your challenge, intentionally living out the *one tangible next* step you committed to in Week 7.

Stewardship is a lifelong journey. The goal of this study was never to arrive at a perfect destination, but to learn how to walk the road of your unique purpose with courage, grace, and a joyful dependence on God. This check-in is a rest stop on that road – a place to look back at the ground you've covered and prepare for the path ahead.

Week 8: Personal Reflection

1) **Your Breakthroughs:** This week's verse encourages us *"not to lose heart in doing good."* Review the *one tangible next step* you committed to in Week 7. How did it go? Describe a specific *win* – a moment where you felt you were able to use your design to serve someone, solve a problem, or bring glory to God in a way that felt authentic and effective.

2) **Your Barriers:** What was the biggest challenge you faced when trying to live out your design? Was it an internal obstacle (such as fear, insecurity, or your *Shadow Side* creeping in)? Or was it an external one (like a lack of opportunity, or misunderstanding from others)? What did that struggle teach you?

3) **Your Growth:** What is one thing you've learned about your design intent in everyday life that you didn't fully understand a month ago? How has your appreciation for God's intelligent design *in you* deepened over the last few weeks?

4) **Seeing the Design in Others:** Over the past month, how has your new understanding of the Fivefold roles changed the way you interact with or show grace to others? Have you been more patient with someone of an opposite equipping? Have you affirmed someone's strengths in a new way?

Week 8: Digging Deeper

1) Based on your reflections on your **wins** and **obstacles**, what is one spiritual discipline (such as prioritizing prayer, accountability, or rest) that could help you persevere in living out your design for the long haul?

2) **Re-read Chapter 11** in *By God's Intelligent Design* (*Discerning, Developing, and Deploying Gifts*). This is the perfect opportunity to refresh your understanding of the stewardship cycle as you continue your journey.

3) **Weekly Takeaway:** Complete this sentence: Looking back on the last month of applying my design, the biggest lesson I've learned is...

Week 8: For Your Ongoing Exploration

1) **Prayer Focus:** Pray for perseverance. *"God, thank You for the progress I've made and for the lessons I've learned from my struggles. Renew my passion to serve You by my design, and grant me the strength to carry on when it's less than easy."*

2) **Intentionality Surfacing:** Perseverance: the Christian life is not a sprint but a marathon. This practice of periodically reflecting, recalibrating, and recommitting is essential for long-term, faithful stewardship. Go the distance this week – push through, especially when you feel like giving up.

3) **Intelligent Design in Action:** Based on your reflections, identify a *New Next Step*. What is one tangible goal you can set for the upcoming month to continue growing in the intent of your design? Write it down and share it with a trusted friend.

4) **Prepare for the Future:** Thank you for completing this study! To help you share this journey with others, a ***(Spare) Equipping Ministry Matrix*** is included in the appendix on page 101. Continue to walk in the beautiful, balanced authority of your God-given design. As you follow the leading of the Holy Spirit, you'll be amazed at how your unique purpose unfolds each time you say, *"YES!"*

Part 3:

Wrapping Up: Encouragement, Conflict Resolution, and Resources

A Word from the Author

Be Strengthened By The Process

Knowing your design is the first step, but the true power of your authentic equipping role is unlocked when it's communicated with a love and humility that makes others eager to receive it. **As you complete this workbook, you are equipped with a new language for understanding yourself and those around you.** This knowledge is a powerful tool – it can be used to build people up with precision and care, or it can be wielded clumsily, causing unintended harm. The difference lies not in the tool itself, but in the heart of the one who holds it.

Knowledge Tempered by Love

Humility and Love are the non-negotiable handles for Kingdom tools. Without love, as the Apostle Paul reminds us, our capacities are nothing more than disruptive noise (1 Corinthians 13). Without humility, our greatest strengths quickly become our *Shadow Side* – things like distancing dictatorship and harsh judgment. **Love** transforms spiritual gifts as life-giving, equipping affirmations. **Humility** ensures that as you learn to see your own design more clearly, you do so with gratitude, not pride, recognizing that every ability is a pure chance to serve.

Honoring the Design in Others

Remember that **everyone is a child of God, and each one of us has spiritual gifts, equipping roles, and Kingdom opportunity.** When you interact with someone, you are not merely observing a collection of behavioral traits; you are witnessing a unique and irreplaceable reflection of a facet of God's own image.

The goal is never to put people in a box ("*You're such a stereotypical Pastoral type*"), but to honor the divine design within them ("*I see the beautiful way God has aligned your heart and gifted you to care for people*"). This posture shifts you from being an observer of human behaviors to being an aficionado of God's innovative genius.

Therefore, **treat people as though you are serving the Lord directly, with Him watching your actions and considering your tone.** This is the heart of true ministry. Jesus made this radically clear when He said, "*...Truly I say to you, to the extent that you did it to one of these brothers of Mine, even the least of them, you did it to Me*" (Matthew 25:40b). Likewise, we are called to do our work "*...heartily, as for the Lord rather than for men;*" (Colossians 3:23b). Every conversation, every act of service, and every moment of showing tolerance to someone with a different wiring is a direct act of worship. It is how we faithfully steward the understanding we've been given.

A Gentle Strength: The Sheep and the Lion

All of this isn't to say that choosing to be a gentle sheep means you can't still be a fierce lion – or even a gentle lion or a fierce sheep! **By all means, walk in that authority with the true conviction of your calling.** The journey of this study is to embrace this necessary tension. The *sheep* in us patterns after the Good Shepherd with a heart of gentle service, compassion, and humility – a posture that offers others safety in our presence. The *lion* in us moves with the courage, conviction, and spiritual authority of our calling. It is the boldness to lead, to speak truth, and to pioneer new ground. Maturity in Christ is not choosing one over the other; it is learning to lead with a servant's heart, to speak truth with profound love, and to care for others with fierce strength.

You have been wonderfully made for a unique purpose. Now, go and walk in that beautiful, balanced authority. Serve well.

On the journey with you,

Adam L. Janowski

Creative Conflict

Navigating our God-Given Differences

When sculpting something into form, sparks often fly. The clash of a **hammer on metal**, the scuff of **sandpaper shaping wood** – these are not frictions to be eliminated, but indicators of progress. In the same way, the resistances you feel when different spiritual equippings interact are not problems to avoid; **they are features of God's intelligent design – our opportunity!**

We were intentionally wired with contrasting perspectives and priorities. He designed the Evangelistic gatherer's focus on the *crowd* to exist in tension with the Prophetic guardian's need for *principle*. He knew the Apostolic pioneering drive for *progress* would clash with the Pastoral nurturing care for the *community*.

Your design is not just about how you view the world; it's also about how others perceive you. These are not accidents; they are the sparks God uses to forge something stronger, more balanced, and more resilient than any single perspective could build on its own.

◇ **As an Individual:** Gain powerful self-awareness that will improve *all* of your interactions. Enjoy learning about your natural tendencies and perceptions.

◇ **With a Partner:** Discover how your differences can become complementary assets, not just recurring tensions. Understand new ways to build each other up as well as how to ease the potential friction in your partnership.

◇ **In a Group:** Learn how your style is experienced by others and how to honor every voice, harnessing the collective power of diverse strengths for a greater Kingdom impact through lasting results.

Your given capacity is perceived differently by those with contrasting equippings. Although sometimes our preferences are easily observable, understanding these subtleties is the key to transforming likely friction into fruitful collaboration. With this guide as your blueprint, let's navigate our designs and the beautiful, balanced, and sometimes combustible ways they can interact.

The Apostolic Lens: Driving the Mission

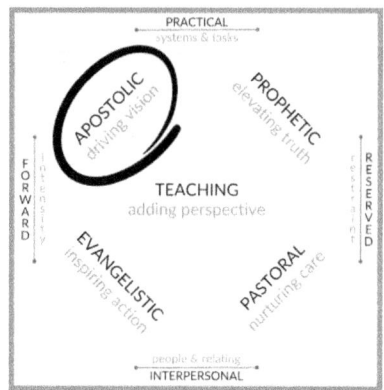

As an Apostolic type, you are the **architect and the general contractor** of God's Kingdom work. You see the end goal, you map the most efficient path to get there, and **you have an innate drive to break ground and start building – RIGHT NOW.** Your focus is on progress, action, and results.

Your Core Conflict: A relentless forward momentum is your greatest strength, but it can also be your biggest blind spot. **Your intense focus on the *what* and the *when* can sometimes overshadow the *who* and the *how*,** forcing predictable frictions with the many who are wired differently than you.

Apostolic ↔ Prophetic: *Momentum vs. Integrity*

This is the classic tension between the bulldozer and the inspector. You see the open field and want to start digging the foundation, while the Prophetic type wants to double-check the survey lines, test the soil, and ensure every permit is in order. **You experience their caution as *red tape*** – the frustrating delays that kill momentum. In contrast, they experience your speed as reckless and overwhelming, fearing you might cut corners on principles for the sake of progress.

◇ *Bridge to Collaboration*: Intentionally honor the Prophetic type's role as quality control. Before taking action, present a plan and ask them, "What potential risks or integrity issues do you see here?" Valuing their input upfront saves you from costly mistakes, prevents rework, and earns their supportive trust.

Apostolic ↔ Evangelistic: *The Mission vs. The Mingle*

This is a core tension between **the strategic plan and the party**. You have the project timeline mapped out, while the Evangelistic type is focused on generating excitement and making sure everyone feels included and energized. **You may see their relational focus as all flash and little substance – a distraction from the hard work.** They, in turn, can perceive your task-oriented approach as cold, impersonal, and dismissive of the very people needed to accomplish the mission.

◇ *Bridge to Collaboration*: Reframe your perspective. The Evangelistic type isn't distracting from the mission; they are **gathering the workforce and boosting the morale for it.** Delegate the roles that amplify people energy to them. Task them with building excitement and communicating the vision in a way that inspires action, freeing you up to focus on the structural execution.

Apostolic ↔ Pastoral: *Progress vs. People*

This is a common friction between the **hard decision and the hurt feelings**. To achieve the goal, you see the objective need to make tough, sometimes painful, calls. The Pastoral type immediately feels the emotional impact those decisions will have on the community. **You may view their concern as being overly sensitive and a barrier to progress.** They, in turn, are likely to feel steamrolled, perceiving your mission-first style as harsh, demanding, and seriously lacking in empathy.

◇ *Bridge to Collaboration*: Treat the Pastoral type as your team health advisor. Before announcing a tough decision, consult with them privately. Ask, "How can we implement this change in a way that best honors and cares for our people?" As your sincerity earns their trust, they will gladly provide the perspective you need to ensure your vision doesn't leave a trail of relational wreckage.

Apostolic ↔ Teaching: *The Decisive Call vs. The Deep Dive*

Obviously, tensions can exist between "**let's decide**" and "**let's deliberate.**" You value the Teaching type's balanced inputs but you grow impatient when their desire to explore the nuance of every perspective slows the commencement. **You're ready for a verdict, while they are still enjoying the deliberation.** You see their process as resistance to progress, while they see your haste as a refusal to compromise.

◈ **_Bridge to Collaboration_:** Frame your requests for input with clear parameters. Instead of asking, "What do you think?" say, "I need to make a decision by Friday. Can you give me your top two pros and cons before then?" This honors their intellectual process while respecting your need for a deadline.

The Apostolic Mirror: *Unstoppable Meets Immovable*

When two Apostolic types collaborate, the result is either exponential progress or explosive conflict. The shared drive is validating, but the potential for competing visions and power struggles is immense. **Success depends entirely on establishing a designated leader and crystal-clear lanes of authority.** Without them, you risk becoming two captains steering the same ship, inevitably leading to a fractured team.

P I O N E E R I N G : *Through Healthy Interactions*

Your role is often to drive the mission forward. Allow yourself to see that the perceived "weaknesses" of other types are actually their greatest strengths. **Prophetic caution, the relational appeal of the Evangelistic, Pastoral empathy, and the Teaching type's clarifying wisdom are the very things that sustain your vision.** Allow moments to pause and intentionally check in on the sentiments of your partners and team. Ask, "How are you feeling about all of this?" and truly listen, seeing their needs not as a distraction from the goal, but as an essential part of it.

The Prophetic Lens: Elevating Truth

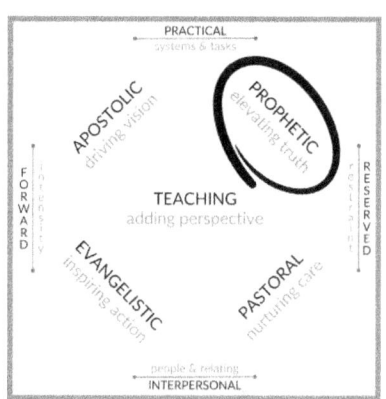

As a Prophetic type, you are the **guardian of integrity and the anchor of truth** for God's people. **You are guided by a deep-rooted requirement that things be correct, principled, and composed.** You instinctively analyze systems and statements, ensuring that the ministry's foundation is solid and its direction is true.

Your Core Conflict: Your unwavering commitment to truth is your greatest strength, providing essential discernment and stability. **The blind spot, however, can be in the colder, matter-of-fact delivery.** Your focus on the precision of *what* is right can sometimes overshadow the grace of *how* it is communicated, causing your insights to be perceived as rigid, critical, judgmental, and distance inducing.

Prophetic ↔ Apostolic: *Integrity vs. Momentum*

Interplay between **the inspector and the bulldozer** allows for tension to build. You see the Apostolic type's rapid pace and instinctively hit the brakes, concerned that their drive for progress might be impulsive and reckless, cutting corners on vital principles. **The Apostolic often experiences your preemptive questions as barriers to progress,** concluding that you'll bog down the mission with analysis paralysis.

◇ *Bridge to Collaboration*: Frame your contributions as risk management that serves the mission. Instead of just pointing out flaws, say, "I am fully behind this vision. To ensure it succeeds long-term, here are three potential issues we need to address first." This aligns you with their goal, positioning you as a wise strategist, not an obstacle.

Prophetic ↔ Evangelistic: *Substance vs. Style*

There's another strain between **doctrinal depth and relational reach**. You hear the Evangelistic type's engaging, accessible message and worry that they are being superficial, potentially watering down the truth to be popular. **The Evangelist, in turn, may receive your clarifying questions as negative and critical**, feeling that you are a joy-killer who stifles the energy needed to connect with people.

◇ *Bridge to Collaboration*: Become the Evangelistic type's partner in credibility. Affirm their knack for approachable interactions and offer to be their content expert. Ask, "How can we share this exciting message in a way that is both powerful and doctrinally sound?" This transforms a potential critique into a partnership.

Prophetic ↔ Pastoral: *Principle vs. Peace*

This is a classic tension between **the hard, necessary truth and amiable tolerance.** You believe that a healthy trajectory requires addressing issues with foundational rules, even when they're difficult to hear. **The Pastoral type feels the immediate emotional pain this can cause and seeks to protect the peace.** You may see them as conflict-avoidant and enabling, while they often experience your directness as a weapon that causes hurt rather than healing.

> ◇ *__Bridge to Collaboration__*: Before delivering a hard truth, consult the Pastoral type. Honor their empathy by asking, "I need to address a difficult topic. What is the most grace-filled way to communicate this so that it leads to healing, not just deepened wounds?"

Prophetic ↔ Teaching: *Conviction vs. Context*

This is the contrast between **a clear verdict and a nuanced view**. You value a firm, black-and-white conviction, but the Teaching type is comfortable exploring the gray areas and multiple perspectives. **You may perceive their comfort with complexity as a lack of firm conviction**, while they can see your definitive stance as overly simplistic and lacking grace for the intricacies of life.

> ◇ *__Bridge to Collaboration__*: Use their Teaching capacity to strengthen your application of truth. Invite their mediating perspective on a core principle: "This is the clear scriptural standard. What context is key to applying it?"

The Prophetic Mirror: *A Fortress of Integrity*

When two Prophetic types collaborate, they optimize an environment for profound stability, security, and meticulous planning. **The mutual respect for process and principle is high.** The primary danger is becoming a closed system that is resistant to change and new ideas, leading to *analysis paralysis* where the collective need for composed certainty prevents timely accomplishments.

G U A R D I N G : *Through Grace-Filled Interactions*

Your role is to be an anchor of truth for the body. Remember that this truth is most effective when it is delivered in love and received with grace. **Permit yourself to see the other types not as compromisers, but as God's partners who make that truth actionable (Apostolic), accessible (Evangelistic), receivable (Pastoral), and understandable (Teaching).** Your wisdom, seasoned with grace after God's own character, becomes the firm foundation on which everyone can safely build.

The Evangelistic Lens: Inspiring Action

As an Evangelistic type, you are the **inspirer and the gatherer** of the community. **You dive into situations with infectious energy, a passion for people, and an eye for exciting potential.** You are the welcoming front door, breaking down barriers and initiate a warm environment where people are drawn in and inspired to take their next step.

Your Core Conflict: Your knack for generating excitement is your greatest strength, generating momentum and growth. **Your blind spot can be a lack of focus on the details and long-term structure needed to sustain that initial energy.** Your passion for relational accessibility can sometimes be perceived by others as foregoing substance for style.

Evangelistic ↔ Apostolic: *The Mingle vs. The Mission*

This is a clash between **people energy and project efficiency**. You are focused on a vibrant, welcoming atmosphere, but the Apostolic type is intent on executing a strategic plan. **They may perceive your relational style as a distraction from the hard work**, while you see their task-oriented approach as overly serious, rigid, and cold to the very people needed for the mission.

⬦ *Bridge to Collaboration:* Channel your inspirational energy into their structured process. Before pitching a big idea, draft a simple outline. Approach the Apostolic and say, "I have a vision for a new outreach that could have a huge impact. Can you help me form the strategic framework to make it a reality?"

Evangelistic ↔ Prophetic: *Style vs. Substance*

There's a core friction between **relational reach and doctrinal depth**. You craft a message to be as engaging and accessible as possible, but **the Prophetic type worries that in the process, you are being superficial and sacrificing truth for popular appeal.** You, in turn, can feel that their constant fact-checking and principled questions act as joy-killers, stifling the imaginative energy needed to connect with people.

◇ ***Bridge to Collaboration:*** Proactively partner with the Prophetic type to establish credibility. Before launching a new initiative, run the core message by them. Ask, "I want to make sure the foundation of this is solid. Can you help me ensure this message is as grounded as it is engaging?"

Evangelistic ↔ Pastoral: *The Crowd vs. The Community*

Shared alignment to the Interpersonal direction still leaves a contrast between **gathering widely and caring deeply**. You are energized by large events and bringing new people into the fold, while the Pastoral type is focused on the quiet, long-term care of the existing flock. **You might see their inward focus as lacking the momentum needed for growth, while they can feel like your high-energy events carry a pace that is too fast** and neglects the deeper, long-term needs within the community.

◇ ***Bridge to Collaboration***: Present a *front door to living room* pathway. Partner with the Pastoral type to ensure the people you gather don't get lost in the crowd. Ask, "How can we offer a great system to make sure the guests from this big event feel personally seen and cared for *next week* and *next month*?"

Evangelistic ↔ Teaching: *Passion vs. Perspective*

This is the tension between **inspirational stories and reasoned substance**. You interact with passion and emotion to move the heart, while the Teaching type communicates with reasoned perspective to foster understanding. **You may find their responses feel limiting, stifling, and draining of your passion.** They, in turn, may feel your enthusiastic presentation lacks intellectual depth and logical progression.

◇ ***Bridge to Collaboration:*** Let the Teaching type provide the *why* that supports your *wow*. Before issuing a passionate appeal, ask the person with the Teaching capacity to help you structure your key points. This adds weight to your message, stimulating a powerful appeal to mind and heart alike.

The Evangelistic Mirror: *A Festival of Possibility*

When two Evangelistic types merge their energies, they generate intense levels of excitement, and many new ideas. **The brainstorming sessions are thrilling and full of possibilities.** The primary danger is a lack of practical foundation; a whirlwind of initiatives may be launched with great fanfare, but few will be sustained long-term without the structure and follow-through that other types provide.

G A T H E R I N G : *Through Grounded Interactions*

Your role is often to generate excitement and bring people through the door. To build a truly lasting community, however, you must learn to value the preferences and aversions of the other equipping types, especially when they're of a different pace and priority than your own.

The structural drive of the Apostolic, the guarding substance of the Prophetic, the long-term care of the Pastoral, and the balanced perspective of the Teaching role are the very elements that turn a crowd into family. See their need for plans and principles not as a hold on passion, but as the wind that gives your sails true direction and purpose.

The Pastoral Lens: Nurturing Care

As a Pastoral type, you are the **empathetic heart of the community**. You read situations through a lens of relational health, safety, and long-term care. **You are instinctively drawn to the well-being of the flock, naturally offering a protective harbor where people feel seen, heard, and valued.** Your focus is on healing, restoration, and maintaining unity.

Your Core Conflict: Your profound capacity for empathy is your greatest strength, supporting the essential bonds of community. **Your blind spot is an uncommonly deep desire for gentle exchange that often leads to conflict avoidance.** In an effort to shield feelings, you shy away from necessary confrontation or hard truths, which can sometimes enable the continuance of unhealthy patterns.

Pastoral ↔ Apostolic: *People vs. Progress*

The heart of this conflict rests right between **emotional support and tough decisions.** You immediately feel the relational impact of the Apostolic type's mission-driven calls, often perceiving their direct, goal-oriented style as harsh, demanding, and lacking sentiment. **The Apostolic, in turn, can view your focus on feelings as overly sensitive and an inefficient distraction from achieving goals.**

◇ ***Bridge to Collaboration:*** Present your empathetic insights as a strategic tool for morale and emotional health. Instead of only absorbing the group's stress, proactively approach the Apostolic and say, "I can sense people are feeling the strain of this new initiative. To maintain morale and prevent burnout, could we include a moment of pause to celebrate a recent win?"

Pastoral ↔ Prophetic: *Peace vs. Principle*

This is the tension between **maintaining harmony and delivering a hard truth.** You value a gentle, restorative approach, while the Prophetic values principled correction. **You often experience their directness as a cold and judgmental weapon that causes hurt.** They may see your desire to protect feelings as being conflict-avoidant, preventing a necessary truth from bringing about true health.

◇ ***Bridge to Collaboration:*** Partner with the Prophetic type on their delivery of truth. Acknowledge the importance of their insight and say, "That is a reality we really need to address. Let's work together to find the most loving and grace-filled way to communicate it so that it can be heard and lead to lasting restoration, not just hurt feelings."

Pastoral ↔ Evangelistic: *The Community vs. The Crowd*

Priorities vary between someone **caring deeply and another gathering widely.** You focus on the long-term, quiet care of the existing flock; the Evangelistic person is invigorated by high-energy events for new people. **You can find their outward focus overwhelming, feeling it neglects the deep needs of those already present.** They, in turn, may feel your inward focus lacks the momentum needed for growth.

◇ ***Bridge to Collaboration:*** Position your capacity as the next step in the Evangelistic process. Introduce a clear *welcome to the family* pathway for newcomers and tell the Evangelist, "Your gathering capacity is amazing! Let's make a great handoff process so I can help make sure those new people find a true home here."

Pastoral ↔ Teaching: *Compassion vs. Clarity*

There's a fork in the road **between sentiment and perspective**. You approach situations with empathy, seeking to validate emotions first. **Teaching, in seeking to add perspective, gently guides the conversation toward understanding and a workable conclusion.** You may feel their shift for a conclusion lacks the compassion a situation requires, while they can feel that discussions with you circle around feelings without ever moving toward a healthy understanding.

> ◇ *Bridge to Collaboration*: Suggest the clarity that comes from their Teaching as the next step of after care. Once you have helped someone process their feelings, you can say, "Now that we've honored the emotions here, what wise, balanced perspective can you offer to help us find a healthy way forward?"

The Pastoral Mirror: *A Harbor of Safety*

When two Pastoral types collaborate, they bring about a restorative environment of profound empathy and mutual care. **The danger is establishing an echo chamber for conflict avoidance.** The shared desire to keep the peace can cause both to shy away from necessary confrontations, leading to stagnation or enabling unhealthy patterns to go unchecked.

C A R I N G : *Through Courageous Interactions*

Your nature is to provide a safe harbor for the flock. True, deep-seated health sometimes requires the forward drive of the Apostolic, the corrective truth of the Prophetic, the outward growth of the Evangelistic, and the Teaching type's balanced perspective. **Consider these other equippings not as threats to peace, but as God's catalysts for maturity.** True and lasting peace is often found on the other side of a courageous but necessary conversation.

The Teaching Lens: Adding Perspective

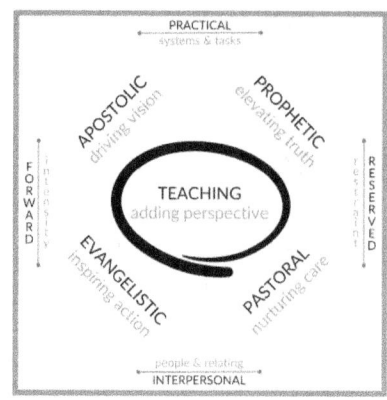

As a Teaching type, you are the Fivefold's **clarifier and mediator**. You are not aligned with any single corner of the matrix; rather, you serve as the vital hub that connects the other four roles. **Your unique ability is to see all sides, understand the nuance, and weave divergent threads into a cohesive, balanced whole.** You are the "*equipper's equipper*."

Your Core Conflict: Your ability to see the complete picture is your greatest strength, but it also introduces a divergence at times. Because your centered position acts as a stable fulcrum, the other, more polarized types perceive your balance from their own unique angle. **Forward types see your caution, Reserved types feel your push for a conclusion, Practical types notice your relational focus, and Interpersonal types sense your objectivity.** This can lead others to see your balance as resistance to their specific directional bias, while you risk getting so satisfied with a clear understanding that you feel little urgency to translate insight into action.

Teaching ↔ Apostolic: *Deliberation vs. Decision*

This core friction is between *let's find the middle* and *let's decide*. You prefer to explore every angle to ensure balance, but the Apostolic is ready for action now. **You may perceive their approach as too single-minded and hasty**, while they grow impatient with your process, viewing it as indecision that slows down the mission.

◇ *Bridge to Collaboration*: Translate your understanding into actionable options. Say, "I can see a few potential paths forward here. Allow me until tomorrow to outline the pros and cons of each one so you can make the most informed decision."

Teaching ↔ Prophetic: *Context vs. Conviction*

There's a resolvable tension between **a nuanced viewing lens and a clear verdict**. You are comfortable with the gray areas, while the Prophetic type seeks a definitive, principled ruling. **You might see their black-and-white viewpoint as overly rigid**, while they may see your balanced approach as a lack of firm conviction.

> ◇ *Bridge to Collaboration*: Frame your role as helping to apply their stated conviction. Say, "You've clearly defined the non-negotiable principle here. Now let's explore the most effective and grace-filled way to apply that truth in this complex situation."

Teaching ↔ Evangelistic: *Perspective vs. Passion*

This is the classic split between a **coherent message and inspirational energy**. The Evangelistic type communicates with passionate stories to move the heart, while you, as the Teaching type, seek to provide the reasoned substance that fosters lasting understanding. **You may perceive their enthusiastic presentation as powerful but lacking a clear intellectual thread.** They, in turn, can feel that your desire to structure their ideas drains the spontaneous energy from their message.

> ◇ *Bridge to Collaboration*: Provide the *why* and *how* that supports their *wow*. After the Evangelistic individual shares an exciting idea, affirm their passion and then offer your help by saying, "That's a powerful message. Let's work together to structure it into a few memorable points so that people can easily remember and share it."

Teaching ↔ Pastoral: *Clarity vs. Compassion*

Conflict resides between **clarifying perspective and compassionate validation**. The Teaching type seeks to gently guide the conversation toward understanding and a healthy path forward. **The Pastoral type insists on a safe space to process feelings without the pressure of a solution.** You see their feelings fixation as a barrier to resolution, and they find your push for clarity as emotionally distant.

> ◇ *Bridge to Collaboration*: Acknowledge the emotional reality of a situation to foster understanding. Before you offer your balanced perspective say, "I can see this is a really frustrating situation." This fosters the trust needed for your clarifying insights to be received and accepted.

The Teaching Mirror: *A University of Understanding*

When two Teaching types collaborate, the result is a rich, nuanced, and intellectually stimulating exploration of ideas. **If they aren't trying to teach each other, the conversation is deeply satisfying as they build on the other's insights.** The primary danger is getting trapped in a cycle of endless discussion that is rich in content but fails to produce a clear, actionable outcome.

C L A R I F Y I N G : *Through Mediated Exchanges*

Your function is to bring clarity and connect the other, more polarized Fivefold equippings. Test yourself in moving from understanding to application (Apostolic and Prophetic). Enhance conversations by validating their thoughts and feelings (Pastoral and Evangelistic) as you offer your well-reasoned perspective. Your balanced wisdom makes the entire body stronger.

The Integrated Body: Where Conflict Becomes Collaboration

The friction between our God-given designs is not a flaw; it is the system itself. *Apostolic* forward momentum prevents stagnation, *Prophetic* anchoring ensures the mission is wise and principled, *Evangelistic* bridges bring new life, and *Pastoral* empathy protects relationships. Bringing the clarity needed to weave these distinct threads together, the centered *Teaching* role serves as *the equipper's equipper*.

Navigating creative conflicts with grace and humility is how a diverse group becomes a unified body that reflects the character of Christ, building itself up in love. **Embrace the sparks. Honor the differences.** In the beautiful tension of life's interactive opportunities, we find not just a better way to work together, but a clearer reflection of the God who designed us all.

Appendix

Additional Products, Content, and Resources for You

It's here in the appendix that we can offer you even more resources to aid your journey of discerning, developing, and deploying your spiritual gifts within your Fivefold equipping roles. We'll start things off with a mini table of contents:

On the next few pages, you'll see how the Authentic Behavior Contrast website offers a suite of tools to help you apply the principles from this book. Whether for personal growth or for building a stronger ministry team, these resources are designed to provide clear, actionable insights.

An Exclusive for Readers of This Book

Receive a **complimentary ministry version** after you get a premium content results report. We replace the ABContrast matrix with the Fivefold equipping ministry background image, saving you the step of transposing the results! **To claim your bonus:** After you complete your ABContrast, we process and upload your premium content results report. Simply reply to that email and request your *"Complimentary Fivefold Version."*

Go Deeper with a Premium Report

For those ready to see the complete picture, our premium ABContrast reports offer a full, in-depth analysis detailing your natural strengths and common challenges. Our all-inclusive ABSOLUTE Plan contrasts all 6 areas of authentic behavior. We detail your natural strengths (God-given capacity), pose your common challenges (the *Shadow Sides*), and provide you personalized, actionable growth strategies. *We also offer laser focused plans for Communication, Influence, Relationship, and Teamwork*

We have three paths to help you get the exact report you need:

For Individuals: (The perfect next step) Receive an in-depth report detailing your likely strengths, common challenges, and actionable growth strategies – in each ABContrast area.

Scan this QR to see our premium content options:

For Coaches and Counselors: Get powerful insights on behalf of your clients, designed to be leveraged in your coaching or counseling practice. When buying two or more login access codes, you can add a group comparison.

For Facilitators, Teams, and Managers: Revolutionize organizational development and team-building by purchasing individual assessments at scale for 2 to 200 people! Add a group comparison for extra insights.

Go to: ABContrast.com/premium and unlock your full potential!

The ABContrast's Companion Guidebook: by Adam L. Janowski

Now that you've completed the workbook, deepen your understanding with the official companion guidebook to the Authentic Behavior Contrast model.

ABSOLUTE HARMONY © is the ABContrast model's official companion guidebook. The current 3rd edition (296 pages) is packed with additional insights about the 4-5-6 of authentic behavior and is available to you now as a digital download. A new, 4th edition will be available in 2026.

- Get the 3rd Edition Download: ABContrast.com/premium/getthebook

- Upcoming 4th Edition formats: ISBN 9798993051659 (paperback); ISBN 9798993051673 (hardcover); ISBN 9798993051680 (ebook).

Share News of The By God's Intelligent Design Series

You've just completed your 7-week study, which means you are now uniquely equipped to help others begin their own journey of discovery. If your first thought after finishing this workbook was, *I know exactly who needs to see this*, this section is for you. We appreciate you sharing this with your friends, family, or ministry team.

Scan this QR to find the book series with our online retail partners:

By God's Intelligent Design **(The Foundational Book)**
Share the foundational book for this study with friends and ministry partners to kickstart their journey. ISBN 9798993051604 (paperback); ISBN 9798993051611 (ebook).

By God's Intelligent Design: The Individual's Workbook
Study your God-given design in a fun, 7-week guided format to move from insight to intentional action. ISBN 9798993051628 (paperback).

By God's Intelligent Design: The Individual's Workbook

By God's Intelligent Design: _The Partner's Workbook_

An 8-week journey for companions, couples, and partners to build empathy, speak a shared language, and turn points of friction into features of a strengthened bond. ISBN 9798993051635 (paperback).

By God's Intelligent Design: _The Facilitator's Guide_

This is an indispensable resource for guiding small groups, church staff, ministry teams, and more through this transformative week-by-week study of their intended purposes. ISBN 9798993051642 (paperback).

Whether you share a single book with a friend or guide an entire team with the _Facilitator's Guide_, you are helping to build up the Body of Christ. If you're ready to take that passion to an even more professional level, your next step is certification.

Get Certified: Practitioner or Affiliate

For counselors, ministry leaders, and coaches, we offer a path to becoming an **ABContrast Certified Practitioner**. We also have a **Certified Affiliate program** for those who wish to earn commissions by sharing these tools in their circles. ABContrast.com/certification

Stay Informed and Engage Others

Our BLOG: Get ongoing inspiration and practical advice on topics like enhancing self-awareness, managing stress, and improving relationships. No account is required and access will always be free: ABContrast.com/blog

Share the Free Assessments: You already know the power of PERSPECTIVES. Share with friends, family, and your small group to start an engaging, memorable conversation. Visit: ABContrast.com/perspectives/   →

Everything Else: For more info regarding the various premium products, or a custom quantity group package quote request, please send an email to: TEAM@ABContrast.com or feel free to message us here: ABContrast.com/contact

The Core Concepts Quick Reference

Name: **Date:**

The following summarizes the core concepts of *By God's Intelligent Design*. Use this quick reference to the **4-5-6 framework** to navigate your own wiring and – **crucially** – to better understand and encourage those around you in their unique God-given designs and Fivefold functions.

The Four Directions of Preference (*Pace and Priority*)

The four directions are arranged as two opposing pairs that reveal our natural instincts of **Pace** and **Priority**. They establish the foundational *how* and *why* behind the core motivations wired into our *multi-faceted* designs.

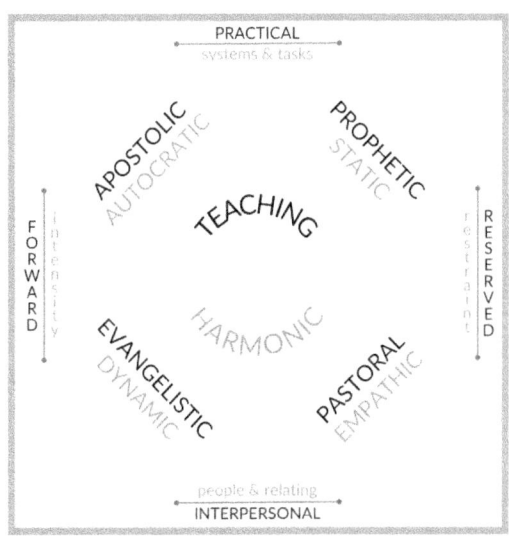

◇ **Forward** (Pace): *A ministry of* **Initiative**. Defined by intensity and speed. Pushing beyond obstacles that stop others, these are the people that take early action, start new things, and drive others to join them.

◇ **Reserved** (Pace): *A ministry of* **Reflection**. Defined by restraint and caution. These individuals pause to listen, process, and carefully consider the subject, context, and path before moving ahead.

◇ **Practical** (Priority): *A ministry of* **Systems**. Defined by logic and objectivity. These types prioritize tasks, procedure, and structured methods in their progression toward measurable outcomes.

◇ **Interpersonal** (Priority): *A ministry of* **Interaction**. Defined by their interactive warmth, inclusive exchanges, and increased sentiment, people of the interpersonal perspective push for everyone's emotional well-being.

The Fivefold Equipping Roles

Specific combinations of the four directions become the five primary functions God uses to build His church. Not prominent titles, these are capacities for serving.

◇ **Apostolic** (Forward-Practical) Core Function: **Driving Vision (*Pioneer*)**

❖ (ABContrast main type: **Autocratic**) Gains new ground by establishing ministries and initiatives. Provides decisive, fearless leadership, especially in high-pressure situations. Focuses on efficiency and results, keeping things moving. *Typical Gifts:* Leadership, Administration, Faith, Missionary.

❖ *Shadow Side: Driven Dictator.* Elevates the mission above all else, treating people as resources by dismissing concerns in favor of momentum. **The Kingdom Pathway**: View people as the mission's true vision. **Key Question for Self-Awareness**: "Is my drive for the mission causing me to overlook the people along the way?"

◇ **Prophetic** (Reserved-Practical) Core Function: **Elevating Truth (*Guardian*)**

❖ (ABContrast main type: **Static**) Provides a grounding force by asking tough questions and ensuring plans are sound. Maintains reliability and consistency, providing a stable foundation for ministry. Offers detail-oriented logic, spotting pitfalls and preventing hasty mistakes. *Typical Gifts:* Discernment, Wisdom, Knowledge, Prophecy.

❖ *Shadow Side: Harsh Judge.* Uses truth as a weapon to condemn and expose flaws, endorsing an atmosphere of fear and judgment over restoration. **The Kingdom Pathway**: Speak the truth in love with tact. **Key Question for Self-Awareness**: "Is my motivation for their restoration, or am I driven by a desire for consequence?"

◇ **Evangelistic** (Forward-Interpersonal) Core Function: **Inspiring Action (*Gatherer*)**

❖ (ABContrast main type: **Dynamic**) Brings high energy and inspiration, motivating others with genuine enthusiasm. Builds social connections and breaks down relational barriers to make people feel welcome. Presents fresh ideas and new approaches, keeping ministry outreach relevant. *Typical Gifts:* Evangelism, Hospitality, Exhortation, Music/Arts.

❖ *Shadow Side*: *Performing Pleaser*. Focuses on superficial numbers and emotional highs, neglecting long-term discipleship once excitement fades. **The Kingdom Pathway**: Value quality roots over quick results. **Key Question for Self-Awareness**: "Beyond gathering a crowd, am I willing to do the slow, faithful work of making disciples?"

◇ **Pastoral** (Reserved-Interpersonal) Core Function: **Safe Harbor (*Nurturer*)**

❖ (ABContrast main type: **Empathic**) Shows deep sensitivity and compassion, noticing and responding to emotional needs. Acts as a gentle peacemaker, sensing tension and promoting reconciliation. Provides steadfast loyalty and a stable, supportive presence for the community. *Typical Gifts*: Pastor/Shepherd, Mercy/Compassion, Helps/Serving, Intercession.

❖ *Shadow Side*: *Appeasing Enabler*. Avoiding conflict and hard truths to pacify feelings, they stifle growth and invite unhealthy dependency. **The Kingdom Pathway**: Provide care with healthy boundaries. **Key Question for Self-Awareness**: "In my desire to care for this person, am I actually preventing their growth by shielding them from responsibility?"

◇ **Teaching** (Centered) Core Function: **Adding Perspective (*Clarifier*)**

❖ (ABContrast main type: **Harmonic**) Acts as a mediator, spotting common ground and building consensus amidst polarization. Brings an anchoring presence, guiding collaborations toward well-rounded outcomes; makes complex spiritual truths understandable and applicable to real life. *Typical Gifts:* Teaching, Knowledge, Wisdom, Writing.

❖ *Shadow Side*: *Proud Elitist*. Uses knowledge to demonstrate superiority rather than to facilitate transformation, looking down on "simplistic" faith. **The Kingdom Pathway**: Pursue transformation, not just information. **Key Question for Self-Awareness**: "Am I preparing this lesson to serve and transform others, or to showcase my own expertise?"

These five equipping roles reveal God's design for our unique purpose. Whether called to clarify, build, guard, gather, or nurture, each capacity is vital but incomplete alone. Together, they are designed to form a balanced and effective body that reflects its Creator.

The Six Areas of Design Application:

Your spiritual capacities are expressed differently across life's distinct arenas. Understanding where and how your design shows up is key to stewarding them well.

◇ **Contemplation (How You Think):** Your inner world of thought, where attributes like Wisdom, Faith, Intercession, and Knowledge take root.

◇ **Connection (How You Socialize):** Your style of building rapport, a common channel for endowments like Exhortation, Evangelism, and Hospitality.

◇ **Command (How You Lead):** How you steward authority and influence, expressed through capacities like Leadership, Writing, and Administration.

◇ **Cooperation (How You Follow):** Your response to authority, reflecting the heart of design functions like Helps, Giving, and Serving.

◇ **Closeness (How You Form Deep Bonds):** Your style of fostering intimacy, where our Care, Hospitality, and Mercy are powerfully expressed.

◇ **Contribution (How You Team with Others):** Your natural role in a group, the practical outworking of the Body of Christ in action.

The Stewardship Cycle:

Stewarding your spiritual design is an active, three-part process that repeats throughout your life's stages and spiritual maturity progressions.

◇ **Discern (Awareness):** Discovering your abilities through prayer, observing your passions, seeking feedback, and experimenting in service to others.

◇ **Develop (Preparation):** Cultivating your talents through intentional practice, study, and mentorship, turning raw potential into refined skill.

◇ **Deploy (Willingness):** Faithfully using your developed strengths in loving, service-oriented, and collaborative ways to build up the body.

The Thermostat Mandate:

God calls us to be *thermostats*, not just *thermometers*. A thermometer passively reflects the spiritual temperature, mirroring the atmosphere. **A thermostat proactively sets the spiritual temperature, changing the environment.** Mature stewardship means using your abilities to effectively introduce elements of God's character into every situation.

Finalizing Your Fivefold Roles

Name: Date:

From Six Area-Specific Results to the Big Picture

You've successfully mapped the six key *rooms* of your life. This is the unique blueprint of your God-given design in communication, influence, relationship, and teamwork. This worksheet is designed to help you step back and see your design in a fresh context: *Foremost* role(s), *Amplifying* role(s), and *Situational* role(s).

Step 1: Tally Your Results

Inspect your completed matrix on page 13 (and the example on page 11). For each of the six areas, identify your unwavering, primary, and secondary equippings.

◇ Did you circle only **one** type in a specific area? That is an **unwavering** result. Place **TWO** tally marks { / / } in the *Primary* tally for that type.

◇ For *primary-secondary* pairing results (two types are circled), the larger circle gets **one** tally mark { / } in the *Primary* column. The smaller circle will also receive **one** tally mark { / }, but it will be placed in that type's *Secondary* column.

Equipping Type	Primary Tally (larger circle)	Secondary Tally (smaller circle)
Apostolic:	_____	_____
Prophetic:	_____	_____
Evangelistic:	_____	_____
Pastoral:	_____	_____
Teaching:	_____	_____

Step 2: Analyze the Totals and Record Your Summary

Based on your analysis, let's find your three tiers of ministry equipping. **This is the core of what talents God has entrusted to you** – your intelligent design blueprint. This reflects a multifaceted design. You should have (12) tally marks.

Note: If and where there's a tie, you simply have more than one Foremost, Amplifying, or Situational role!

◇ **Find Your Foremost Role:** The equipping type with the most tally marks in the **Primary** column is your principal equipping. Write it down.

   o My *Foremost* Equipping Role(s):

◇ **Find Your Amplifying Role:** Of the remaining types, the one with the highest **combined** total (Primary + Secondary tallies) is your **Amplifying** equipping.

   o My *Amplifying* Equipping Role(s):

◇ **Identify Your Situational Roles:** Any other types that received tally marks are your **Situational** equippings.

   o My *Situational* Equipping Role(s):

Congratulations! You now have a clearer picture of the beautiful and complex way God has designed you. Remember that Communication (internal and external), Influence (extended and received), Relationship, and Teamwork are all different facets of God's Intelligent Design in your life. Keep this summary handy as you continue your lifelong journey of discovery.

Reflecting on Your Results

Name: Date:

Your 8-page PERSPECTIVES downloads are filled with high-value content. Consider the single most important insight within each of life's six *rooms*. This exercise will serve as a valuable snapshot of your initial reactions to your results.

Contemplation (Thinking): Your report sheds light on your inner world. What's one discovery that surprised or confirmed something about how you process ideas internally?

Connection (Speaking): This report describes how you build rapport. Pull one phrase from the report that you feel accurately captures your natural social style.

Command (Leading): When it comes to taking charge, the report details how you influence others. What key insight did you gain about your natural leadership tendencies?

Cooperation (Following): Now consider how you receive influence. Which statement from your report best explains how you respond when others are in charge?

Closeness (Relationship): In the intimate room of relationship, your design for forming deep bonds is revealed. Write down one truth from the report that resonated with your heart.

Contribution (Teamwork): Finally, your role in a group effort comes into focus. What is the most helpful piece of advice your report gave for maximizing your effectiveness on a team?

The Big Picture: Looking at all six reports together, what's the most important realization you made about the beautiful, multifaceted way God has made you?

From Creative Conflict to Collaboration

Name: _____ *Date:* _____

The Fivefold roles are designed to work together in harmony, producing an effective and balanced body. This two-part worksheet helps you turn relational friction into fruitful collaboration. **First**, you'll consider a key group collaboration in your life to better understand its collective strengths and potential blind spots. **Second**, you'll use those insights to navigate a specific point of friction, which can turn a potential conflict into an opportunity for growth and alliance.

Part 1: Mapping Your Group's Design

Visualize the collective design of an important group in your life, such as your family, small group, or a work team. By mapping out the likely equippings of each member, you can better understand the group's natural attributes and learn how to navigate its strengths and struggles with wisdom. Follow steps A, B, and C:

Step A: Populate Your Group

Name of Group/Collaboration: _____

Their initials (including yourself): _____   _____

_____   _____   _____

_____   _____   _____

_____   _____   _____

_____   _____   _____

Step B: Draft the Collective Design

Base this on your understanding of the Fivefold, as well as your observations. On the next page, write the initials of each person by the main type that represents their primary function. This is an exercise in appreciation, not judgment.

◇ **Apostolic (Pioneer):** The visionaries, starters, and the ones who drive new projects. ***Who?***: _____

◇ **Prophetic (Guardian):** The question-askers and standard-keepers who ensure things are in order. ***Who?***: _____

◇ **Evangelistic (Gatherer):** The promoters and welcomers who bring energy and people into the mix. ***Who?***: _____

◇ **Pastoral (Nurturer):** The caregivers and peacemakers who protect inclusivity and emotional health. ***Who?***: _____

◇ **Teaching (Clarifier):** The mediators and explainers who bring understanding and balance. ***Who?***: _____

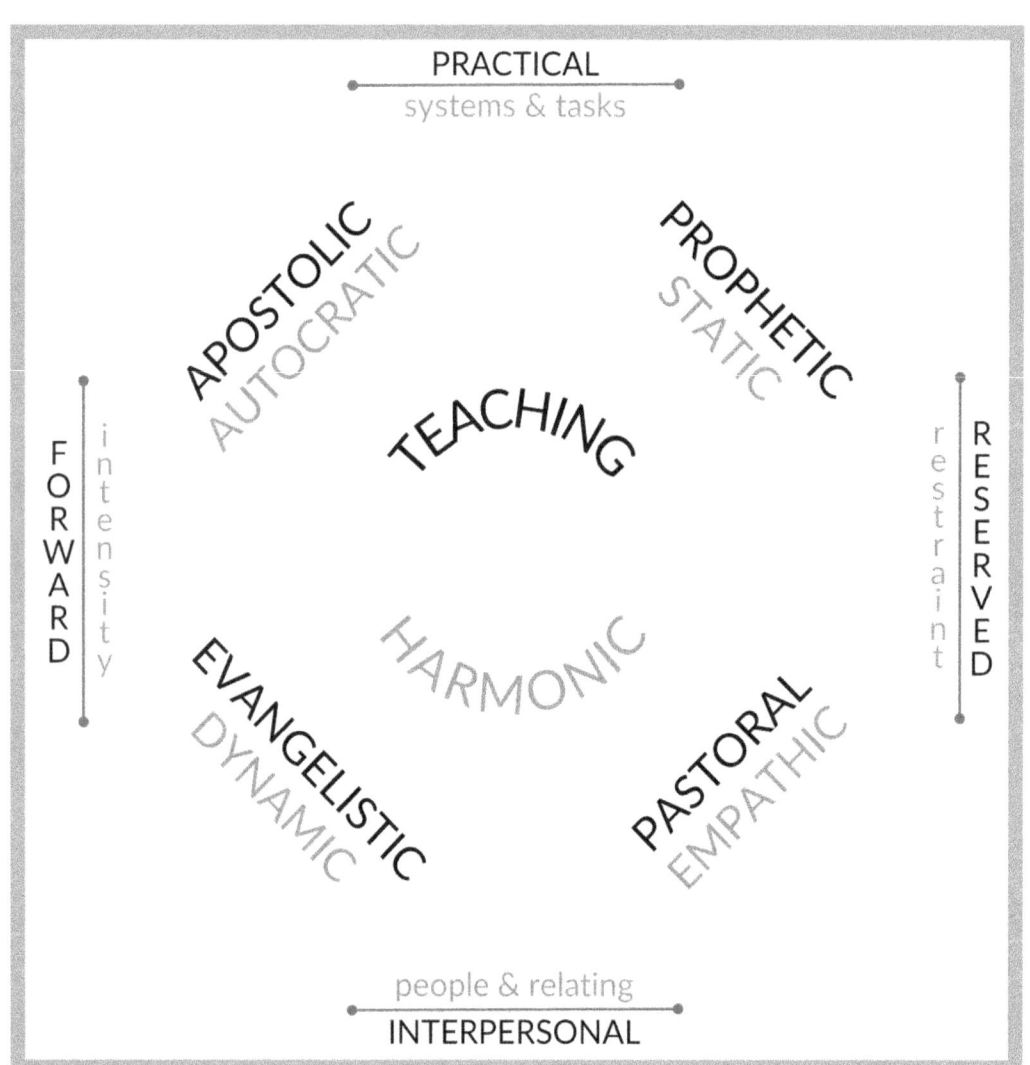

Step C: Analyze the Group Map

Look at your completed matrix and reflect on your group's collective design. **What are our obvious alignments?** (Which quadrant has the most people? What does this group do well?) **Where are our potential blind spots?** (Which equipping roles are not well represented? What important perspectives might we be overlooking?)

Part 2: Navigating a Specific Relationship

Now, apply what you've learned to a specific relationship where you experience recurring tension. This will help you prepare for a difficult conversation or gain a deeper understanding of the perspective gap.

Step 1: Identify the Situation and Lenses

The Person: _____

My Foremost Equipping Type Lens: _____

Their Likely Equipping Type Lens: _____

Our Recurring Tension: ("It feels like we always clash over finances...," "We have different approaches to deadlines," etc.)

From *By God's Intelligent Design: The Individual's Workbook*, by permission, ©2025 Adam L. Janowski

Step 2: Gain Insight and Draft an Action Step

Using the *Creative Conflict* guide in Part 3 of the workbook, find the *Key to Healthy Interaction* for **your** primary type. Based on that key, what is one specific, different action you can take to honor the other person's design and move from conflict toward collaboration?

My Action Step: Plan out an action step. ("I'll start our next budget conversation by explaining the heart behind my logical plan, thereby affirming my Pastoral spouse's desire for a compassionate approach," or "I will ask for my Prophetic partner's analysis of the risks before pushing for a quick decision," etc.)

The Circle Back: How did it go? Even if the result was less than optimal, what did you learn? **Consider their perspective too.** How do you think the other person experienced this new approach? What did you observe in their reaction that was different from your usual interactions?

This is what it's all about – fostering collaboration amidst natural conflict. Ask God to guide you in these matters. Ask Him to reveal your design to others, and their design to you – through His eyes. Keep this worksheet. Make copies of it. Use it as a trusted tool the next time you face the inevitable, God-given opportunity that creative conflict provides.

Navigating My Shadow Side

Name: _____   **Date:** _____

The first step to freedom is seeing our struggles clearly – not with shame, but with the grace-filled courage God provides. Use this worksheet to prayerfully examine your own work (Galatians 6:4) and draft a personal plan for stewarding your strengths with wisdom and humility.

The Inspection: Identifying My *Shadow*

Regarding Chapter 10's content, prayerfully consider which *shadow* expressions seem to show up when you are under stress, feeling insecure, or even operating in an undeveloped facet of spiritual maturity. **Reflect on a specific time this *shadow* tendency emerged.** What was the situation, outcome, and impact on others?

If Your *Shadow* Is...	Your Pathway Is...
☐ The Driven Dictator (**Apostolic**)	*View People As The Mission's Vision*
☐ The Harsh Judge (**Prophetic**)	*Speaking The Truth In Love With Tact*
☐ The Performing Pleaser (**Evangelistic**)	*Quality Roots Over Quick Results*
☐ The Appeasing Enabler (**Pastoral**)	*Caring With Healthy Boundaries*
☐ The Proud Elitist (**Teaching**)	*Transformation, Not Just Information*

The Remedy – My Plan for Grace and Growth

Look Inward: Willing Self-Awareness

◇ **My Triggers:** What specific situations, stressors, or uncertainties tend to activate this *shadow* tendency in me? (tight deadlines, feeling unheard, fear of failure, etc.)

◇ **An Early Warning Sign:** What is one thought or feeling that can serve as an *early warning sign* that my *shadow* is emerging (such as "I feel the need to control this," or "They just don't get it," or "I'm starting to feel resentful.")?

Look Outward: Deep Accountability

◇ **My Accountability Partner:** Who is one trusted person (mentor, spouse, friend) I can offer permission to speak into my life about this specific *shadow* tendency?

◇ **The Question I Need Them to Ask:** What is one specific, direct question I can ask them to pose to me ("Have you seen me act like a dictator this week?" "Was my feedback in that meeting harsh or helpful?" or "Am I enabling that person out of a fear of conflict?" etc.)?

<u>**Look Upward:**</u> Cultivating the Spirit's Fruit

◇ **The Antidote:** The Fruit of the Spirit is God's remedy for our *shadow* behaviors. Which fruit is the most direct antidote to my primary *shadow* (**Patience** for the Driven Dictator, **Gentleness** for the Harsh Judge, **Faithfulness** for the Performing Pleaser, **Self-Control** for the Appeasing Enabler, or **Humility/Love** for the Proud Elitist)?

◇ **Intentionality Surfacing:** What is one practical spiritual discipline I can intentionally practice this week to cultivate that fruit? ("To build patience, I will practice the discipline of silence for 10 minutes each day," "To develop gentleness, I will write one unsolicited note of positivity each day," etc.)

From Inspection to Intentionality

Remember, this plan is not a contract for perfection, but a compass for your journey. It is a practical tool for partnering with the Holy Spirit, Who is pleased to provide you the grace for today and the strength for tomorrow. Refer back to this resource as needed, not as a reminder of your struggles, but as a testament to your courageous commitment to walk in freedom. Stewarding your strengths with humility is one of the highest forms of worship, allowing you to more fully reflect the beautiful, balanced character of Christ in every area of your life's capacity and spiritual giftset.

Additional Space for Your Notes

Linking Your Design to Specific Gifts

Name: _____   **Date:** _____

You have discovered your primary Fivefold equipping roles – the broad *how* of your service. Now, it's time to connect that blueprint to more of the specific spiritual attributes God gave you. Chapter 16 of *By God's Intelligent Design* provides a rich glossary of these endowments. This worksheet helps you identify which of those gifts resonate most and understand how they function within your unique Fivefold design.

Prayerfully read through the list below and on the next page. As you read, check the gifts that cause the strongest sense of resonance in your spirit.

Specific Spiritual Gifts: My Notes:

☐ *Administration*

☐ *Apostle (foundational) / Apostolic (role)*

☐ *Artist / Craftsmanship*

☐ *Celibacy*

☐ *Discernment (Distinguishing of Spirits)*

☐ *Evangelism / Evangelistic*

☐ *Exhortation (Encouragement)*

☐ *Faith*

☐ *Giving*

☐ *Healing*

☐ *Helps / Serving*

☐ *Hospitality*

☐ *Intercession (Prayer)*

☐ *Knowledge*

☐ *Leadership*

☐ *Mercy / Compassion*

(Gifts Continued)	*My Notes:*

☐ *Miracles*

☐ *Missionary*

☐ *Music*

☐ *Pastor / Pastoral / Shepherd*

☐ *Poverty (Voluntary)*

☐ *Prophet / Prophecy / Prophetic*

☐ *Teaching / Teacher*

☐ *Tongues (Speaking and Interpreting)*

☐ *Wisdom*

☐ *Writing*

Your *Foremost*, *Amplifying*, and *Situational* roles were tallied on page 87's *"Finalizing Your Fivefold Roles."* Match your broader list of spiritual gifts as follows:

1) Which spiritual gifts fully align with your **foremost** equipping role(s) and why are they instrumental in serving others?

2) What specific spiritual gifts are integral to your **amplifying** equipping roles? (Think about past experiences, passions, or moments where you felt energized and effective.)

3) Which spiritual gifts are only put to use **situationally**, such that it's less common that you'll be operating in these ones? Why do you appreciate them?

(Spare) Equipping Ministry Matrix

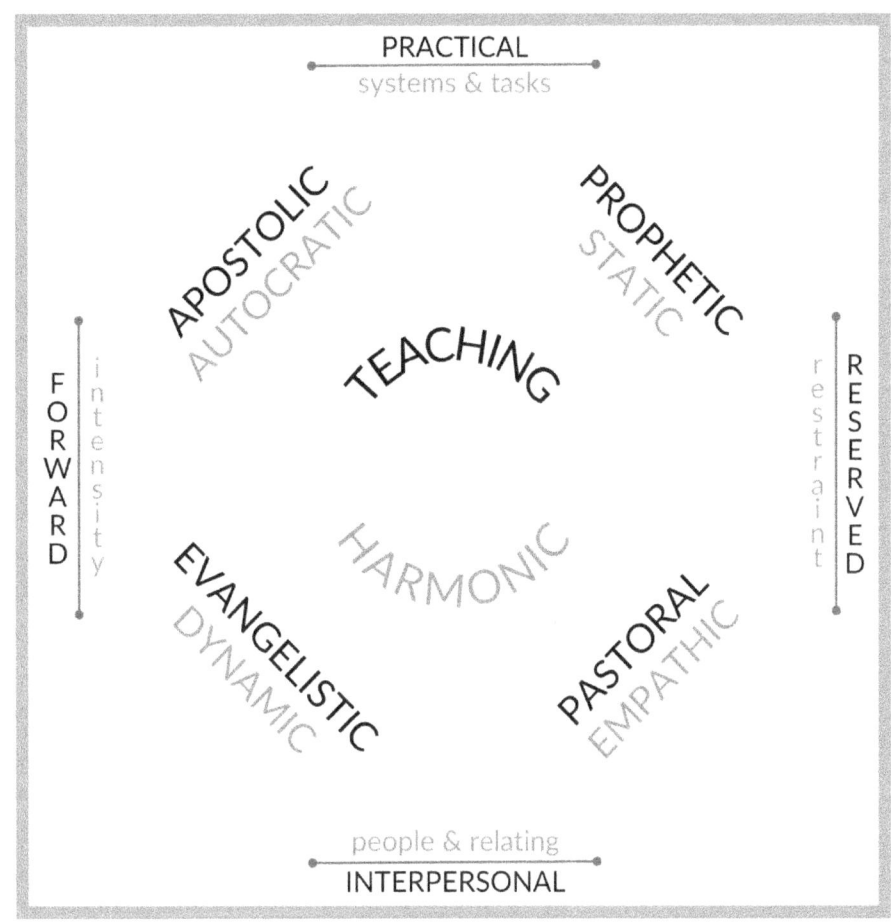

From *By God's Intelligent Design: The Individual's Workbook*, by permission, ©2025 Adam L. Janowski

Name: _____ Date: _____

Thinking/Socializing Equipping(s): _____

Leading/Following Equipping(s): _____

Relationship Equipping(s): _____

Teamwork Equipping(s): _____

Your Design's Central Theme and Noteworthy Findings:

Additional Space for Your Notes

www.ingramcontent.com/pod-product-compliance
Lightning Source LLC
Chambersburg PA
CBHW082249120626
46555CB00009B/3017

9798993051628